Edward S. Ellis

The Rival Scouts

A tale of the last century

Edward S. Ellis

The Rival Scouts
A tale of the last century

ISBN/EAN: 9783337299392

Printed in Europe, USA, Canada, Australia, Japan

Cover: Foto ©ninafisch / pixelio.de

More available books at **www.hansebooks.com**

THE
RIVAL SCOUTS.

A Tale of the Last Century.

LONDON AND NEW YORK
GEORGE ROUTLEDGE AND SONS.

THE RIVAL SCOUTS.

CHAPTER I.

> Ever deeper, deeper, deeper,
> Fell the snow o'er all the landscape,
> Fell the covering snow and drifted
> Through the forest and the village.—HIAWATHA.

NIGHT in the wilderness! a night of tempest, of darkness and of death.

Back to the gloomy days of the eighteenth century, when the North American colonies were the dependencies of the British crown. Back one hundred years, through the rise, the glory, and, shall we say, decline of the American nation? Back to that time of which no living being holds the most shadowy remembrance: it is there the pen of history leads us.

It was the dead of winter, and for thirty hours the snow had fallen without intermission. Great flakes came drifting noiselessly downward, loading the trees with a burden which many a one was unable to bear, filling up the interstices until it lay in enormous depth upon the leaves and ground. Silently it fell upon the cold, placid river, that as silently absorbed it out of sight, as if it could never receive its full of the feathery pureness; silently it gradually wrapped every thing in its folds, until nothing, over the immense area, served to relieve the terrible monotony that held reign.

Here, in the depth of this awful solitude, what is there to arrest attention?

Could we have penetrated to the centre of that vast forest which stretched along the southern shore of Lake Erie, a century ago, we might have discerned a person laboriously making his way forward on this tempestuous night in January, 1763. Nothing but his upright position and forward movement would have identified him as belonging to the human creation. There was no swinging of the arms, or motion of the head, nothing, except that plodding lifting and placing of his feet, as he patiently pushed his way through the tempest.

That he was a man of nerve, of endurance and of woodcraft, was evidenced by his being abroad on such a night as this. Even the indomitable aborigine scarcely stirred from his wigwam. Plunder, treachery, or hatred could not suffice to bring him forth. But Basil Veghte, for over ten hours, had resolutely forced his way through the snow, that was whirled in blinding eddies around his head, and almost bore him to the earth from its extreme weight. Thirty years of frontier life had given him the strength of the buffalo, the endurance and sagacity of the panther, and the iron constitution that scarcely succumbed at the most terrific strain under which it could be brought.

But, at length, he halted beside the immense trunk of an oak, which reared its head so far above, as to be invisible in the darkness.

For a moment the man stood silent and thoughtful, as if listening for some expected sound; but nothing disturbed the dreadful stillness of the great solitude, except the faint soughing of the wind, and the far-away roar of Lake Erie. Leaning a perpendicular mass of snow, which enclosed his rifle, against the tree, he scraped his feet so vigorously over the ground, that he speedily cleared a space several yards in extent. He next began breaking limbs from the surrounding trees, and continued the employment, until he had heaped up a large pile. After this, numerous branches were strewn upon the ground, and the leaves were overturned, until an armful of crisp, dry vegetation was produced. This was carefully placed beneath a mass of dry twigs, a flint and tinder was produced, and the difficult and delicate task of kindling a fire was begun. The experience of Basil Veghte at this kind of business gave him skill, and scarcely a minute had elapsed ere a great, roaring, crackling fire blazed up against the old oak, and sent a flood of light among the grotesque limbs and trunks around. Shaking the snow from his blanket, he spread it upon the branches behind him, and, lighting his pipe, sat down to enjoy himself.

Ah! the warm glow of those cheeks, the power of those lungs, the sparkle of those keen grey eyes, and the rugged health of that matchless body! What would the dyspeptic man of to-day not exchange for their possession?

"Quite a smart chance of a storm!" muttered the man, as he whipped the snow from his leggins, and stretched them toward the fire. "I s'pose I might have kept on till morning, but then, what's the use? I'll get to the fort in time enough. Christie isn't in any special hurry to see me; and if he is, he can come out in the woods to meet me."

A dull boom, distant but distinct, came faintly through the storm to the ears of the hunter.

"There goes the evening gun of the fort! They're late with it to-night, but it proves that all is right, and so I may take a comfortable sleep. It was so long time coming, that I began to fear I hadn't heard it at all, which would have proved that I had lost my way. Howsumever, its sound tells me I'm just where I thought I was, which is all right again."

The man smoked slowly and steadily, gazing abstractedly into the fire, and betraying by his manner that his enjoyment was as keen as if he were seated by the fire-place in some protecting cabin in the settlement. Occasionally he would turn his head, and peer into the darkness, as if he would penetrate its length, and breadth, and depth, and search out what might be there concealed.

"It can't be any one else is abroad to-night," he continued, as he brought his gaze back to the fire. "Pontiac himself could'nt trail me on such a night as this, and I do n't think he would be tempted to come forth, even if I was promised him; and yet the old chap *would* like to lay hands on me!" chuckled the man, with an expression of satisfaction on his rough face.

Again he turned his head, and shading his eyes with his hand from the glare of the fire, looked searchingly forth.

"At any rate it won't do any harm to keep Sweetlove by me!" he added, as he arose and took his rifle from its resting-place.

"It's qua'r how I feel to-night; it's just that same way that come over me, the night Wilkins and I was set on in the woods, by the Indians, and he got wiped clean out. Poor Wilkins! I made a plunge into the snow-drift, and got off, with a couple of holes in my legs, while he hardly knowed what killed him."

This time Veghte rose to his feet, and once more cast a searching glance around. He was about to resume his seat, when he could not avoid a start at discerning the movement of something a few rods away.

"Who comes this way to-night?" he demanded, holding his rifle in a position to fire at an instant's warning.

"A friend."

The reply did not throw the woodman off his guard.

He remained standing until the stranger emerged from the gloom into the circle of light, and when he saw beyond all doubt that he was a white man, rather short in stature, and slightly given to corpulency, Veghte scanned him narrowly as he came up. Taking his position by the fire, the stranger shook the snow from his garments, but neither offered to shake hands, although there was every appearance of cordiality in their manner.

"Ruther a qua'r night for a man to be tramping out of doors," remarked Veghte, in an inquiring tone.

"I think so, too. I'd sooner have expected to meet a comet abroad in the woods, than to have come across your camp-fire."

"I couldn't believe there was a man walking the woods upon such a night as this, beside myself, and now that I've found you're abroad, I'll stake my life that there isn't a man, white or red, that is stirring out doors, within fifty miles."

"A purty safe ventur'," remarked his companion, removing his coon-skin cap, and disengaging the enormous mass of snow that crowned it. "A purty safe ventur'," he added, replacing the cap, and giving a sort of general convulsion, that sent the snow flying from him, as if he had been a great shaggy dog.

"We're alone in these parts, that's purty sart'n. I had just made up my mind that I should have to camp out as best I could, when I caught sight of your fire, and as I observed, it *did* give me such a start as I haven't had in a long time."

All this time, Veghte stood with his keen eye fixed upon the stranger, as if he would read him through. While he avoided that open appearance of suspicion in his manner, that under the circumstances would have been insulting, he still manifested a prudent reserve, as if he were not entirely satisfied with the aspect that affairs bore. He did not hesitate long to ask the question that had been in his mouth from the moment he first caught sight of the stranger.

"You called yourself a friend, but I didn't hear the name—that is, if you did give any."

"I didn't give any," remarked the stranger, placing his hands carelessly behind him, and turning his back to the cheering fire.

The cool assurance with which this was uttered disconcerted Veghte, somewhat accustomed as he was to encountering all classes of men. Withal, it touched him.

"Let's hear the name, then, as I don't s'pose you can have no objection to giving that."

"No, don't know as I have," said the man, in a musing tone, but still refraining to yield the desired information. "But, then, what's in a name, Basil Veghte?"

The woodman was once more taken aback at this proof that he himself was so well known to the new-comer Waiting scarcely a moment, he added:

"Whether there is any thing or not in a name, don't matter; but you can take your ch'ice, and do one or t'other of two things. Give your name or just leave this place, and camp somewhere else."

The stranger looked at him and laughed.

"Basil, don't you remember Brock Bradburn?"

Veghte scanned him narrowly a moment, and then made answer:

"Don't think I ever heard the name."

"Guess you didn't; for I never did till just now."

"Do you mean to say that isn't you?"

"I rather think I do."

"And do you mean to say you don't intend to tell me who you are?"

"S'posen I do?"

"I've given you your ch'ice; you can leave me alone by the camp-fire. You came uninvited, but you needn't go away in that manner."

"S'posen I don't choose to go away at your bidding," said the stranger, with a half-smile and a deep look in his eye. That of Veghte glittered dangerously, at these annoying words.

"If you'll be kind enough not to *s'pose* any thing about it, but just to say yes or no, you will soon learn what is to be done."

"How does the name of Zechariah Smithson suit you Basil? It isn't very melodious, I know, but do you think you could give me the right hand of welcome on it?"

"If it's your real name, and your intentions are good, you are welcome to my fire, and to my blanket."

"I'm obliged, but I have a blanket of my own. I see you're smoking—you'll allow me to do the same."

With an obeisance, as if to say, "By your leave," the stranger plucked a brand from the fire, and holding it up before his face, proceeded to light his pipe. While thus engaged, the flare of the brand illuminated his features in a far better manner than the camp-fire had done. In fact, he had been careful to avoid letting the full flow of light upon his face, from the first; and now, his action, instead of being simply intended for that of lighting his pipe, had the appearance of being done for no other purpose than that of affording the suspicious Veghte—what he manifestly desired—a full view of his features. We need hardly say that the opportunity was improved to the utmost. The woodman scrutinized the beetling brows, the keen dark eyes, the short nose, the full face, and the straggling beard that covered the lower portion. He was sure he had encountered that same countenance before, under some peculiar circumstances, and he strove to the utmost to recall the time and place. He ran back over the experience of his life for the last few years, and thought of the principal of the many exciting scenes through which he had passed. But it was all of no avail.

He now, as a last resort, repeated the name of Smithson, again and again, to assist his memory. The continued repetition of the name satisfied him of one thing: it was the same as its predecessor—an invention.

This conviction seemed to put Basil Veghte in an unenviable frame of mind. He was in earnest when he presented his ultimatum to his visitor, and he was now determined that it should be enforced.

The man had taken his seat upon the branches, first having spread his blanket, and he was now in the full solace of his pipe. The calm, abstracted gaze that he threw into the fire, revealed, beyond question, that he was in a contented frame of mind. Veghte was upon the point of speaking, when his companion saved him the task.

"Snowing as hard as ever! 'Pears to me this is about the greatest snow-storm that ever caught me out. If it keeps on all night, it will be no small piece of work to reach the fort in the morning."

"What fort are you going to?"

"Presq' Isle, up on the lake."

"That's the point toward which I've been aiming for the last three days."

"Yes, I know; you wanted to get there to-night, the same as myself, but made up your mind that it was hardly worth while, just the same as I did."

"'Pears to me you know a mighty sight," returned the woodman, considerably exasperated.

"Not a great deal. Howsumever, there's one thing in which I *am* ahead of you—although I have to say it instead of you."

"And what can that be?"

"I know your name, and you don't know mine."

"Didn't you give me your real name?"

"I knew yours from *remembrance* only, while you don't seem able to place me, although you've had a better look at my face than I had at yours. No; I didn't give you my real name," said the visitor, coming back to the question that was asked him. As if aware that he was treading upon the edge of a volcano, he added:

"I've just been trifling with you, Basil, for the fun of the thing. I'll now give you my real name; it is HORACE JOHNSON."

CHAPTER II.
"Methought I heard a voice."

THE name sounded familiar to Basil Veghte, but, for a moment, he was unable to recall the circumstances under which he had heard it before. All at once he recollected that this man had been his companion two years previous in a voyage along the shore of Lake St. Clair, when they were set upon by a canoe-full of Chippewas, from whom they had great difficulty in escaping.

"Strange that I didn't recollect you," laughed Veghte, as he offered his hand. "I did feel as though I had seen your face and heard your voice before, but I couldn't tell where, if my life had depended on it. What made you keep me waiting so long?"

"Just for the fun of the thing. I knowed you the minute I set eyes on you. I kept my face kind of shady like at first; but there was no need of that, as you couldn't make it out when I held the brand before me. Let me see; it is a good two years since we had that trip in old St. Clair, isn't it?—and that is the last time we were together, too, wasn't it?"

"Two years last autumn. You have changed considerably since then, Horace."

"Think so? I fancied not. I can't say that there's the least difference in you. You've got that same lock of hair over your temple that I remember so well. Where have you been during these two years?"

"Mostly at Presq' Isle; though it's now full three months since I've been in the fort. I've spent a great deal of the time at Michilimackinac, and not a little at Fort Sandusky, St. Joseph and Ouatanon."

"Singular that we've never met since then. I have been at all three of them forts, and am just now from Fort Sandusky."

"When did you leave that post?"

"In October—near the middle of the month."

"I was there in November, for over a week. You've taken more time than I have to reach the fort."

"I did not hurry, as there was no particular need of it."

"Neither did I until I found this storm preparing, when I did make a little extra tramping in the hope of reaching the fort to-night. But it isn't the fastest way of walking when the snow is two feet deep."

The two were now seated before the fire, each reclining upon his elbow, smoking his pipe, and glancing occasionally into each other's faces, as their conversation proceeded. At other times their gaze was fixed upon the fire, which seemed to burn all the more gloriously from the furious storm that raged unremittingly around. The gigantic branches overhead, although loaded to the utmost, still caught the descending flakes of snow and held them suspended, like the sword of Damocles, which needed only the slightest tremor to bring the miniature avalanche down upon their heads.

"Still snowing," remarked Johnson, as he shaded his eyes and gazed out into the darkness. "If it keeps on till morning, we shall have a good tramp before reaching the fort."

"I shouldn't wonder if it kept up all day, too. It began like a regular storm that meant to last. You remember what a fall of snow we had last year on Christmas day. It lasted for the best part of a week," said Veghte, in an inquiring tone.

"I think I shall never forget that as long as I live. I was about a dozen miles from Fort Sandusky when it began, and didn't get in until it was all through. I had been out hunting, and in the afternoon got a shot at a bear that only wounded him, so that, instead of showing fight, he took to his legs and run, with me following after him. I could see by the blood on the ground that he was hurt pretty bad, and I expected every minute to see him keel over or turn round and wait for me. But the confounded brute kept running and running till it got dark. I had followed him so far that I was a little wrathy, and made up my mind not to give him up, if I could help it. The last glimpse I got of him, he tumbled down a sort of hollow, and I catched my foot and tumbled heels over head after him.

"When I got up, I saw nothing of the bear. I listened, expecting to hear him tearing through the bushes, but all was still, which made me think that likely enough he had gone under at the last. I couldn't feel certain, howsumever, so I hunted around awhile. But it was no use; there was nothing to be seen or heard of him.

"About this time I saw it had begun to snow, and I came to the conclusion that the best thing I could do was to start up a fire and take it comfortable until morning, for, although the snow was falling, it was a great deal colder than it is to-night. We men who live most in the woods are always ready for such times, and I didn't have much difficulty in getting a good, rousing fire started. I took a tree, every bit as large as this oak, as my fire-place, and it made things pleasant, I can tell you.

"Wal, I lit my pipe, and stretched back, and went to thinking. I don't know why, but try as much as I might, I couldn't get the thoughts of that bear out of my head. And such queer ideas, too, they would have made an Injin laugh. I fancied him to be the grandfather of some large family that were expecting his return that evening to preside over a grand feast. And I pictured him sitting at the head of the table, like some old British General, and telling his visitors how I had insulted and tried to kill him, while he had spared me only that he might take the better revenge. Then I heard them all take a vow that I should be followed and made to wipe out this insult. I don't know how much further the fandango would have gone, for just then I raised my eyes, and there, within six feet of me, stood the wounded bear.

"Yes, sir; I was scared. I believe the hair on my head rose straight up, for the worst of it was, I had been fool enough to let my rifle be on the ground while gathering the brush for the fire, and had forgot all about it. But, as I looked at the bear, I seen the barrel shining under him, so that it wasn't a safe task to attempt to lay hands on *that* just then.

"The brute had his mouth wide open, and there was plenty of blood on his jaws, so that I hadn't much reason to hope he held any good opinion of me. I s'pose he'd slapped down behind the tree to die, but found he wasn't hurt so bad as he thought, and so concluded to come around and see what the fire meant, and to square accounts with me afore he went under.

"It must have been that he was scared full as much as I was, for he stood growling and looking at me for two or three minutes, without stirring. If I'd had sense enough to have kept still, likely he would have gone off without touching me; but I was a complete fool just then. Finding I couldn't lay hands on my gun, I must rise up so as to get a better look at the animal. While I didn't move, he didn't seem to know exactly what I was, and held off; but the minute I stirred, he seemed to understand how everything was.

"With a bigger growl than ever, he commenced coming toward me. Just then I reached forward, catched up a brand and slammed it in his face. He couldn't stand that, and backed out again, but it wasn't five seconds afore he was in his old place, watching me with a look that plainly said he meant to have me, if he had to wait till daylight.

"Getting up close enough to the fire to make it safe, I begun thinking harder than ever. It didn't take me long to discover that all the wood I had gathered would last just about two hours more—maybe not so long as that. And then what was I to do?

"I looked around me, and found that the limbs of the tree could be reached by jumping, so when I couldn't do any better, I could make my way up the tree; but then that was big enough for the bear to climb, and he might take it into his head to make further trouble. About this time, too, I came to the conclusion that I had made a purty bad shot—hitting the bear and allowing him to get off with such a little wound.

"If I could only get hold of my rifle I could very soon stop this kind of fun. But just there, you see, was the difficulty. The bear was squatted right on it, and it was rather dangerous to undertake to shove him off. Howsumever, there isn't any animal that can stand the fire, so I concluded to gather a good rousing torch, and make a charge on him.

"I picked up the best-looking brand that I could find, and swung it around my head several minutes to get it into a good, roaring blaze, and then, setting up the tallest kind of a yell, made a tearing rush at the brute. Possibly I might have got my gun, if I hadn't stubbed my toe just then, and fell down so hard that the torch flew clean out of my hand. It didn't take me long to scramble back to the fire, but quick as I was I just saved getting clawed to pieces.

"By this time the camp-fire began to get low, and I seen it couldn't be long before I'd have to shift to other quarters. I meant to keep on the ground as long as I could, for I didn't fancy roosting in the tree on such a cold night, until I should have to do it.

"But things begun to look so doubtful, that I made a spring upward, and, in a twinkling, was up the tree. Afore I went to the top I looked down to see whether my friend was going to follow me. But it must have been that I happened to jump at the minute when he didn't have his eye on me, for I could see him moving his head around as if he was searching for me.

"There wasn't any telling how soon he would scent me out, so I crawled well up among the limbs to wait till morning. It was rather uncomfortable, I tell you, to sit on one of those limbs in the cold, with the snow falling on you;

but there wasn't any thing else to be done, and so I made up my mind to bear it.

"The first thing I knowed I begun to get very cold and sleepy. It came on me so fast that, in a few minutes, I tipped off the limb, and came right plump down within two feet of the bear. I was wide awake enough by this time, and sprung up and catched one of the half-dead embers to defend myself. Whirling it over my head, it instantly blazed up, and I stood ready for my black enemy.

"The bear didn't stir, or make a growl. I waited a minute or two, and then went up closer. He was dead and stone cold. I pulled my rifle from under him, gathered more wood, fixed up my fire, and then examined the animal. I had hit him in the heart and he had bled to death, though how he kept up so long I could never understand. I think like enough—"

At this point Basil Veghte made a warning signal with his finger, and, falling flat on his back, lay in the attitude of attention. Johnson imitated him, and for the space of five seconds, neither seemed to breathe. Finally, Basil carefully resumed his sitting position, and said:

"I heard something when you was speaking."

"Nothing but the wind."

"So I thought at first, but it came twice, and was too plain to be mistaken."

"What did it sound like?"

"Like the cry of some one in trouble. It sounded far off in the woods, perhaps a quarter of a mile away."

Johnson looked meaningly at the face of his companion.

"Don't you know what animal makes that sound, Basil? Haven't you never heard it before?"

"I know what you mean. I've heard a painter too

often to mistake him. A painter screams out like all fury, but this wasn't any such sound as that."

"You said it was a good ways off, and that may have made it sound different."

Veghte shook his head impatiently.

"Do you s'pose I've lived thirty years in the woods to make such a mistake?—There, by heaven, it is again!" he exclaimed, excitedly, springing to his feet and looking out in the darkness. But he might as well have sought to penetrate the solid trunk before him with his vision, as to reach a dozen rods into the snowy gloom around him. "Did you hear it?" he asked, turning upon his companion, who was still stretched upon the ground, imperturbably smoking his pipe.

"I heard *something*, but I ain't sure but what it was the wind. Just listen how it moans through the tree-tops over-head."

Veghte glanced half angrily at him, as if he did not understand his unimpassioned manner.

"I tell you, Horace Johnson, there is some one else besides us in these woods, and whoever it is, he is in trouble."

"P'shaw!" laughed his visitor. "You're foolish, Basil! What could bring 'em out on such a night?"

"What brought *us* out?"

"It is our business; that's what we're made for, to be abroad in the woods on such a night as this."

"And are we the only persons south of Lake Erie that have that business to do? I can't understand what you mean by feeling so careless about it," said Basil, in a reproachful manner.

Johnson curled his lip contemptuously.

"S'pose some one *is* in trouble—what have you to do with it?

"What have I to do with it! What had I to do with giving you permission to squat down there by the fire?"

"That's a different thing. If any one comes to us to-night, we'll take 'em in and give 'em a seat by the fire, and I shouldn't mind letting 'em have a whiff at my pipe. But s'pose that person is a quarter or ha'f-mile away, what have we got to do with him?"

"We've got to help him out."

"*You* may, but *I* don't; that's settled."

"S'posen some one has been cut up by the red-skins, and is left dying in the snow—"

"He'll have to die, that is, if he can't stand it till morning. Basil, have common sense. Don't you see it's snowing harder than ever? How are you to hunt up a person in these woods, when you can't see a foot afore your face after you get away from the fire? What obligations have you, not to run the risk of losing yourself, but to lose yourself to help one who, like enough, doesn't want your help?"

"I don't look at it in that way. I ain't lost so easy as all that. I've tramped too much in the woods not to be able to find my way back to the camp-fire."

"You couldn't on such a night as this."

"Why couldn't I to-night, as well as any other night?"

"Snow and darkness overhead, and snow under your feet."

"Couldn't you shout or fire your gun to guide me?"

"Yes, I might do that," replied Johnson, after he had taken a moment to digest the new idea.

"Wal, do it then, for I'm going. Hark!"

Faint but distinct came a wild, tremulous wail, as if some being far removed from them was in the extremity of agony.

"What direction did that come from?" inquired Basil Veghte.

"I made it from yonder," said Johnson, pointing in precisely the opposite direction from the one in which Veghte was sure he heard the sound.

"That can't be," said the other, in amazement. "It sounded every time from yonder."

"You're mistaken," said the other, confidently. His assured air decided Veghte to wait a moment to make himself certain. A few seconds later the strange sound was repeated from the point indicated by himself.

"There it is again, and it is the voice of a woman! Fire your gun or shout occasionally, so that I can't make a mistake in my way," were the parting words of Veghte, as he plunged into the darkness, in quest of that unearthly wail that was borne to them upon the midnight wind.

CHAPTER III.

> I knew not, I, what weapons he chose,
> What chief he followed, what badge he wore.
> BISHOP BURGESS.

THROUGH the blinding storm, that whirled in eddies around his head; through the darkness that was absolutely impenetrable; through the snow that lay fully two feet deep, pressed Basil Veghte, in quest of that wild voice that had rung out to him upon that terrible December night, from the very depths of the great wilderness.

When he had advanced a hundred yards, he looked back for his camp-fire. Not a trace of it could be discerned.

"Pretty dark—pretty dark," he muttered, as he pressed on; "and the snow does come down as if it wasn't the intention to leave any up above. Whew! but it is more like work than play to make a fellow's way through this."

A moment later, despite the caution he used, he ran full against a tree, and, turning to the left, encountered another with equal violence. Nothing disconcerted, however, he pressed on as resolutely as before.

"'Tisn't very pleasant to be barking one's nose against these trees; but then—hello! there's that voice again."

Although of great courage, the woodman could not avoid a start and a thrill, as the unearthly sound wailed out upon the air within a few rods of him. He stood perfectly motionless a moment, and then thought rather than spoke:

"That *is* a woman's voice, as sure as my name is Basil Veghte. What can it mean? She all alone in the woods at such a time as this!"

Almost any person would have called out to attract the attention of the one whom he was seeking. Veghte could have done so with the certainty of being heard, before penetrating thus far in his search. But he was too cautious a man to do such a thing. His trained ear detected in the sound that had just reached him the unmistakable evidence of its being the voice of a female Indian!—a fact which warned him to be exceedingly cautious in whatever he did. Suppose the whole thing were a skilfully-arranged artifice to entrap him—was it not possible that the man whom he had left behind at the camp-fire was an instigator of the project? Not daring to risk an open encounter, not wishing to shoot him down from the gloom of the wood, what better stratagem could be devised to secure possession of his person!

These thoughts flitted rapidly through the mind of the woodman, as he stood listening for further evidence of the being that had called him forth in this singular manner. He waited several moments, turning his head in different directions to make sure there were *no other* persons in his immediate vicinity. He had taken a step or two forward, when he caught the sound of a low, monotonous, chant-like song, whose significance he recognized in an instant.

"Heaven save me! that's the Death-Song!" he ejaculated, in genuine astonishment. "There's no treachery there, but there's some one in trouble. Hello!"

The chant continued, as if no interruption had occurred. Thinking perhaps he had not been heard, Basil repeated his call.

"Hello! I say there, don't you hear me? HELLO!"

The last call penetrated far through the blinding storm, so that there could be no question about its reaching the ears for which it was intended.

"There's no stopping an Indian when he starts his Death-Song," exclaimed Veghte, impatiently. "And she appears to have got a reg'lar start."

He now pushed on, and, in a few moments, stood within a half-dozen feet of the woman who was giving utterance to that solemn dirge, rendered doubly solemn by the peculiar circumstances surrounding. Peering eagerly forward, he could discern the outlines of a large tree-trunk, and standing out against it he either saw, or fancied he saw, a human being. A step or two further satisfied Veghte that he was right in his first supposition. By this time he was considerably out of patience that the woman should continue her chanting, when she could not fail to be conscious of the immediate presence of a stranger.

"Shut up!" he called; "or I'll lurch you over! What's the sense of your bawling out in that manner, when nobody wants to hear you! Shut up, I say, or I'll make you."

Had he spoken to the wind, it would have had as much

effect as did his words upon her to whom they were addressed.

"You won't stop, eh? We'll see, then."

With which he unceremoniously stepped forward and placed his broad palm square over the mouth of the young squaw. This, of course, checked all musical demonstrations for the present. Basil Veghte next proceeded to feel of her arms and hands, and then of her feet, to acquaint himself with the amount of clothing with which she had protected herself against the severity of the weather.

"Freezing to death, by heaven! It wouldn't take much longer to finish you, my young gal. Hey! what's that on the ground? Her blanket, as sure as I live. We must have a fire here, that's sart'in. Don't you stir, or I'll lam you," he said, in a warning manner, as he proceeded to clear away a space and collect fuel for a fire. "I don't know as she could run, if she tried, the poor creetur' is so near gone." Then he added, in a louder tone, thinking it possible that he might have been unheard:

"Don't you undertake to slip away, for I've got my eye on you; and just as sure as you do, I'll fetch you one."

It didn't seem to occur to the good-hearted woodman that the Indian could be sensible of the impossibility of his "having his eye" upon her, when neither was visible to the other, nor the emptiness of the boast that he would "fetch her one," whatever was meant by that dreadful threat. However, he deemed it advisable to throw in a wholesome warning every moment or so, to keep her reminded of the terrible fate in store for her, in case she attempted to brave his authority.

"I'm an awful man when I'm excited, and I shouldn't advise you to get me excited, for there's no telling what I might do. Like as not I'd kill you before I'd take time to consider. Hello! you ain't slipping away there, are you?" he suddenly called out, dropping his bundle of sticks and rushing toward her. "No, no, poor thing, you've dropped, have you?" he added, in a pitying tone, as he found her in the snow, and wrapped her blanket carefully about her Hold on a minute till I get the fire started, and I'll tend to you."

A few moments later he had started a vigorous fire. At the first flare of the flame, he picked up the suffering being as he would have raised an infant, and narrowly scanned her. She was an Indian scarcely yet out of girlhood, of handsome features, with the brilliant black hair and eyes that characterize her race. She was clad quite warmly, her ankles being protected by serviceable leggins, and her arms by a deer-skin covering, made for that purpose. Still these were insufficient to protect her upon this dreadful night, even if she had not cast away her shawl or blanket. A strange thrill ran through the iron frame of Basil Veghte, as he gazed down in the immobile face of the sadly-suffering creature in his arms, and he was sure he had seen those features before, or else they bore a strong resemblance to some one that he had met. But there was no time for sentimentality, as, beyond all question, a short hour more only was needed to place her out of the reach of all hope. His first proceeding was to rip the leggins from the ankles, and to examine her feet.

"Just what I was expecting—*freezing!* Purty-looking feet and ankles for all that," he said, as he began rubbing them with snow. So violent was this operation that, in a few moments, he forced an exclamation of pain from the almost inanimate creature. "That's the talk," he exclaimed, with a chuckle of delight. "There's more sense in that than in singing that outlandish gibberish. Yell a little more, won't you? It does a feller good to hear that. The blood is beginning to come back in these little feet. Let me wrap my blanket around 'em, and I'll give them plump arms a turn."

He gave the arms several "turns," with such effect that the girl cried out again and again with pain. Not heeding them in the least, Basil continued his manipulations until assured that he had re-established the benumbed circulation.

"I wonder if that nose don't want a twist or two," he added, as he took the end of that delicate member between his thumb and finger. "Feels cold as an icicle, but there isn't any trouble with that. I guess she's in a fair way to do purty well."

Satisfying himself that she was thoroughly wrapped up in the two blankets, he deposited her upon the ground, somewhat after the fashion that he would have handled her had her age been about one year.

"Women is queer things," mused the great-hearted woodman, as he gazed upon the bundle before him, "and I never knowed much about 'em. I've got a good old mother, somewhere out east, and a sister, too, if she ain't dead."

He paused at this moment to brush the mist that overspread his eyes, at these reminiscences, but shortly resumed:

"Yas, women is queer things, and they've been a great trial to me, for when I get to thinking on 'em, I'm sure to get 'em all twisted up—that is, twisted up in my head. I've never seen a woman with whiskers—that's another queer thing about 'em. Wonder why they don't have whiskers, like us men? S'pose 'cause they wouldn't know how to shave themselves. But, then, they might get some one to shave for 'em—it's queer!"

The mystery was too great to solve, and he accordingly abandoned it.

"The women have long hair, that's something else that's queer. That bothered me a good many years, but I got at the reason of it at last; it's 'cause they let their hair grow. I s'pose mine would get as long as theirs, if I'd only give it time."

The severe mental exercise through which Veghte labored to attain this result, could not fail of bringing its own reward. No disciple of the schools ever rejoiced more thoroughly at triumphing over a problem in Euclid, than did he, at having conquered this perplexing difficulty. He grinned with a kind of novel delight, and then looked at the face of the Indian girl, whose dark eyes were fixed upon him with a strange meaning, that filled him with a vague uneasiness.

"Can you talk English?" he asked, addressing his question directly to her. "'Cause if you can, I'd like to ax you a few questions. Can you talk?"

The fixed look which she turned upon him was the only notice she took of the question.

"Come, say something, or I'll fetch you a side-winder, that'll make you holler!" said he, raising his hand in a threatening manner. Basil Veghte would have been burned at the stake rather than have harmed a hair of the poor creature's head, and it is not necessary for us to say that he only made the pretence to force a word from her. The girl, when she saw the uplifted hand, gave a reproachful, terrified look, that went to the heart of Veghte—such a look as the deer in its death agony sometimes casts upward in the face of the exultant hunter.

"God forgive me!" he exclaimed, catching her up in his arms. "You might know'd I wouldn't harm such a poor critter as you be. I only done it to scare you."

The girl made a struggle, as if the restraint were disagreeable, and a singular feeling of embarrassment passed through him—a feeling that he had acted foolishly in catching her up in the impulsive manner that he did. He laid her back by the fire, and just at that moment felt as if he would he were a hundred miles deeper in the forest—anywhere out of sight of those black orbs gazing so fixedly at him. All at once, she found utterance, and spoke, energetically:

"Go 'way!"

He started at these words, and, for a moment, failed to note their unmistakable meaning in the wonder that he experienced at hearing one speak in his own tongue that he deemed knew nothing about it.

"Go 'way? What for? Do you want me to leave you?"

"Go 'way!" she repeated, with increased energy.

"And leave you here to freeze to death?"

"Go 'way!" she added, as determinedly as before.

"No; I'll be hanged if I will."

At this juncture a peculiar feeling of uneasiness took possession of Veghte, and he began to suspect there was a deeper meaning in the words of the girl. He recalled the singular suspicion he entertained upon approaching this spot, and he looked inquiringly toward his charge, as if expecting some further revelation from her. But she, observing that her commands had no effect, ceased speaking, and looked at him with a mute, appealing look, that told Basil, plainer than words could have done, that his life was in peril at that very moment!

The adventures of the night, up to this time, warned him that he need experience no astonishment at whatever might occur. The consciousness of this impelled him to approach still closer to the Indian, and, bending over her, he asked, in a suppressed whisper:

"What do you mean, gal? Speak, and don't fear. Is there any red-skins around, that are after me? You're an Injin yourself, but you can't want to harm me, after what I've done."

"Go 'way! go 'way!" she repeated, looking straight into his eyes, and refusing, through ignorance or stubbornness, to utter any other words.

"Shall I leave you here?"

She probably failed to understand his question, for she could have no reason for refusing to reply to this.

"I'll go and take you along!" muttered the woodman, catching up the girl, and plunging away in the darkness. The fire by this time had nearly smouldered itself out, and he had taken scarcely a couple of steps, when he was wrapped in the impenetrable gloom of the storm and night.

There was a feeling of relief, at the consciousness that whatever enemies might be in the vicinity, they certainly were on equal terms with himself. Fairly free in the broad woods, he asked only equal terms of his foes, let their color be white or red.

As he pressed onward, his thoughts were exclusively engaged in attempting to conjecture the meaning of the strange circumstances of the evening. The reader may suspect that this was too laborious an undertaking, when the question regarding the opposite sex was so perplexing; but the woodman, to speak figuratively, was now upon his own ground. He considered the matter in all its bearings, and the result was no result. A young Indian girl freezing to death in the heart of an American wilderness, on such a tempestuous night—her curiously urgent desire for her friend to hasten away—the two events for the present were irreconcilable.

From this train of thought, Veghte was aroused by the consciousness that he was travelling entirely at random. No skill in woodcraft could enable him to make his way to a given point in the woods on this memorable night. With this, also, came a feeling of wonder that Johnson had not discharged his rifle, as he had warned him to do. His search had been extended longer than either could have expected at the first, and the report of his gun should have been heard long since.

Veghte finally became annoyed and somewhat angered, when he discharged his own gun three different times without eliciting any response. He had exercised considerable caution in his movements, and was morally certain he could be at no great distance from the camp-fire.

"That fellow must have heard me! He's such a queer one, there's no telling what he means. I can't feel much friendship toward him, but I can use him right, if he only serves me the same way. It can't be that he's gone to sleep—"

A dull, glimmering light caught the eye of Veghte, a few rods to his left, and he discovered at once that he was in close proximity to the camp-fire, which he had been seeking. A few rapid strides, through the obstructing snow, and he deposited his precious burden beside the fire which he had first kindled.

CHAPTER IV

> The storm-wind is howling
>   Through old pines afar;
> The drear night is falling
>   Without moon or star.—E. H. WHITTIER.

"WHY didn't you fire your gun, as I told you?" demanded Veghte, as he turned toward Johnson, who had just risen to a sitting position.

"What under heaven have you got there?" asked the latter, staring at the mysterious bundle.

"Why, a critter that was just freezing to death, and would 'av' freezed, if I'd done as *you* told me to do."

"A woman, too!" exclaimed the man, seemingly unable to recover from his amazement. "If that don't beat all. Hello! she's alive!"

"Alive! of course she is; what's to hinder?"

At this point, the girl so far disencumbered herself of the blankets in which she was enveloped, as to allow her to free her arms, and take a sitting position.

"Keep them things around you!" said Veghte, in a warning manner, "or you know what I'll do—no, I forgot, I frightened you once, and I won't do it again. But don't you take them blankets off, or you'll freeze to death ag'in. See here!" added Veghte, turning toward his first acquaintance, "didn't you hear my gun?"

"B'lieve I did hear something, but wasn't sure what it was."

"Didn't, eh? Didn't you know your own gun?"

"Yes; I b'lieve so," returned the other, with a complacency that was doubly annoying.

"Why didn't you fire it then, and save me tramping all around the woods, trying to find you?"

"Guess you didn't tramp much; thought it would do you good to hunt awhile in the dark, you was so anxious to get off."

"Didn't you intend to shoot at all?"

"Wal, I s'pose I might, by daylight, if you hadn't come in before then."

Veghte looked unutterable things, but hardly dared to trust himself to speak. He gradually toned down, and became mollified enough to renew the conversation upon a different subject.

"Ain't this the queerest thing you ever heard on, Johnson? It's too much for me to get to the bottom of."

"Bottom of what?"

"The manner of this gal being found as she was."

"How did you find her?"

"Why, standing ag'in' a tree, freezing to death."

"How do you know she was freezing to death?"

"Hangnation! how do I know any thing? You're acting like a fool, to-night."

The object of this outburst simply smiled, and resumed:

"You see I want to know all about it. Do you think the gal herself thought she was freezing to death?"

"What was she chanting the death-song for, if it wasn't for that?"

"Was she doing so?"

"Yes, she was, and was nearly through, too."

"That settles the matter, then. She wouldn't 've thought her last sickness had come, if she wasn't purty near it."

"She couldn't have got to that place alone in the woods could she, in this storm?"

"I don't know why she couldn't. Maybe she come there before the storm."

"Do you s'pose she would have come alone?"

"I don't s'pose anything about it. She might have done so, and then she mightn't. I think it likely some one come with her."

"And why did they leave her alone?"

"Purty hard to tell; maybe they weren't far off."

The hint thrown out in the last remark struck Veghte forcibly, and for a few moments his vacant gaze into the fire showed that he was absorbed in thought. Finally he looked up.

"If they was near by, would they have let her freeze to death?"

"Maybe they done it to punish her for something."

"What! such an innocent-looking gal as she? You needn't tell me that."

"But you know these innocent-looking gals are sometimes the most dangerous creatures."

"I didn't know that; women is queer, ain't they? It must be hard to understand 'em."

"'Tis for *some*," replied Johnson, with meaning emphasis. "They never bothered me much, howsumever."

"If they left her there by the tree, what did they let *me* take her away for?"

"That's the strange part of it; it might be that they know'd she couldn't help dying in the storm, and so they went off and left her by herself."

"I can't think it is any thing like that. Johnson, you can talk Injin, can't you?"

"Yes; what if I can?"

"Talk to her; ask her questions; let's find out every thing about her."

" Have *you* asked her any thing ?"

" Yes, but she doesn't seem to understand English."

Johnson gave a quiet laugh.

" Pshaw! she understands it as well as either of us. Don't you see how she is watching us? There hasn't been a word said that she hain't knowed all about it, as well as you or me."

" Why under heaven doesn't she talk, then?"

" 'Cause she don't want to, I s'pose, and if a woman gets it into her head that she ain't a-goin' to do nothing, you may kill her afore she'll do it."

" Is that so?" asked Basil, in the most unfeigned amazement.

" True words as ever I spoke!"

" Women *is* queer things!" he sighed. " Now, if it was one of us men—"

" We'd act just the same way, wouldn't we?"

" S'pose we would, come to think on't, so they ain't so very queer about that, after all. But then if a feller had toted me through the snow and storm, as I did her, 'pears to me I'd answer any decent question."

" Maybe she don't thank you for it."

" She isn't an Indian, then. Look at them dark eyes; don't they speak her thanks?"

" I ain't heard 'em, maybe they did, though. They're black as the night around us, and shine like them coals of fire."

" You just ask her something in the Injin tongue, to be sure whether she understands us or not."

Johnson did as requested, demanding her name. The question was barely out of his mouth, when she said, " Mariano!"

" Mary Ann, did she say?" asked Veghte, in considerable surprise.

"Mariano; a purty good name for an Injin; shall I ask her something else?"

"Yes, do; ask her how she came to be left there alone."

Johnson did as requested, but received no reply, nor could he induce her, by any means in his power, to open her mouth again; and at length, with the philosophical observation that "women is queer things," Veghte advised him to give over the attempt, and allow her to sleep, if she preferred to do so.

For the space of ten minutes or thereabouts, no word passed the lips of either. Veghte remained smoking and gazing into the fire, when, as a sudden thought presented itself, he lifted his head to speak. As he did so, he saw Johnson gazing at the girl and she at him, with a look that startled him. The moment he stirred, the eyes of his visitor flitted to the fire, toward which he looked, as if he were in a brown study, unconscious of the presence of any one around him.

Basil was at a loss to understand the meaning of what he had just witnessed. It looked as though the two beings around him were acquainted, and were exchanging secret signals. The thought presented itself so forcibly, that he asked:

"Johnson, you've seen that gal before."

"What if I have?"

"Why didn't you tell me, when I brought her here?"

"Why would I tell you that, when I didn't know her myself?"

"Don't you know who she is?"

"Mariano, I b'lieve she said was her name."

"Don't you know where she came from—who she is—and the meaning of her being left in the woods?"

"How should I know that?" laughed Johnson. "I've

traveled considerably among the Injins, and may have met this gal somewhere. She looks at us both, so powerful, that we might think she knowed us. 'Pears to me I have seen her face afore, but *where*—that's the thing."

"I wish you could recall it, for I'd mighty like to know all about her; 'pears to me I never wanted to know any thing as much as I do to understand all about her."

"I see you're interested very much," said the other, with a significant look, that sent a strange feeling through the woodman. "'Sh!" he added in a cautious whisper; "she's going to sleep!"

The great, dark eyes had closed, and slumber, sweet and peaceful, was descending upon the poor young Indian. Sorely indeed did she need it, for her exposure and suffering had been sufficient to crush again and again any one of a different race from her own.

The two woodmen forbore speaking, and almost held their breath, for fear of disturbing her. Both fixed their looks upon her, until they saw, by the closed eyelids and regular breathing, that she was locked in a refreshing sleep.

It was now beyond midnight. The fire was kept burning brightly, for sufficient fuel had been collected to last until daylight. The snow seemed to fall more rapidly than ever, the great feathery flakes filling the air and gradually increasing the depth of snow to a formidable extent. If it continued at this rate, the dawn of morning would find it impassable for ordinary people, although Basil Veghte experienced no apprehension on this point.

"I wonder whether she's hungry," he ventured to whisper 'It's likely she must be, don't you think?"

"Likely enough, for all I can see."

"Poor thing! why didn't we think of it?"

"What good would it have done us to think about it, when we haven't any thing for ourselves?"

"I've a piece of good venison," replied Basil. "It isn't much, but if she could stow it away, she's a bigger pig than I think she is."

"She's an Injin, and can stand hunger without grumbling."

"It isn't 'cause she's an Injin, it's 'cause she's a *woman!*" said Basil Veghte, in a mysterious whisper. "They're *queer* things, you know."

"What time of night is it?"

"I s'pose it must be after midnight."

"Do you propose to get any sleep yourself?"

"I ain't partick'ler; just as you say."

"Well, I'm in for it; and if we expect to get any, we must be at it soon. There's enough wood to last till morning."

"Yes, plenty, if used as we ought to use it."

Veghte arose and stooped over Mariano to see that she was properly protected for the night. He then carefully placed a quantity of branches and limbs upon the fire, so as to make it burn as long as possible without attention.

"When it gets too low I'll be sure to wake up," said he; "though it ain't likely any of us will freeze to death, for the weather don't strike me as being very cold."

"Too cold for *her*. I'm glad you're apt to wake, for when I get fairly at work sleeping, it takes a good deal to stop me."

The two now prepared themselves for slumber. There was but one blanket between them, on account of Veghte having given his to the Indian. Even this they could have dispensed with, were it not for the annoying fall of snow. Stretching themselves upon the branches, they drew the blanket over them, and in ten minutes both were sound asleep.

About an hour later, Basil Veghte, from some cause or other, awoke. He regained his consciousness so slowly that, in the bewildering state of his senses, he never could be really certain of the cause that aroused him. His impression and belief were that it was the voices of persons speaking in an undertone. Stretching out his hand, he found that Johnson was absent, and then, throwing the blanket from his face, he arose to the sitting position. Had he exercised the caution that ordinarily characterized him, he might have settled a matter of which he remained in doubt to his dying day.

As he arose, Johnson was in the act of throwing wood upon the fire, and Mariano, the Indian girl, was apparently in as deep slumber as an hour before, when he had lain down. Still he could not free himself of the impression that they had been conversing together.

"Hello! you awake?" remarked Johnson, as he turned around.

"Yes. What are you doing?"

"I found the fire was getting low, and thought I wouldn't disturb you, as the cold had waked me up."

"Hasn't Mary Ann—the gal there—hasn't she been awake?"

"She? When?" asked Johnson, turning around and looking at her, as if he had not been aware of her presence until this moment.

"If I was ever certain of one thing, it was that I heard you and her talking together."

Johnson indulged in one of his characteristic laughs.

"Do you s'pose she'd speak a word to me, when she wouldn't notice you, who prevented her freezing to death?"

"It don't look reasonable that she would, but then women is *queer* things, and it is hard for one to understand 'em."

"There, I guess that fire won't need much attention afore morning," remarked Johnson, as he returned to his primitive couch and lay down again. "Let's see if we can get an hour or two of good sleep."

There were unpleasant suspicions in the mind of Basil Veghte—enough to keep him awake for an hour or more. He could not free himself of the belief that Johnson and the Indian girl were acquainted with each other, and that he knew more of the cause of her being left alone in the woods than he chose to reveal. It may be that there is a subtle magnetism in our natures that sometimes warns us against those who are evilly disposed toward us. Basil Veghte recalled that, upon his first encounter, several years before, with the man beside him, he could experience no cordial friendship toward him, although the circumstances, at the time, were such as would naturally have made the strongest enemies the best of friends. And now, upon his coming to the camp-fire, on this night—coming in this great solitude, when he believed himself entirely alone—he could not really welcome him. He wished him away. His presence boded no good.

As might have been anticipated, in the midst of these reveries Basil Veghte dropped off into the land of dreams, and was not disturbed for several hours. As before, he was aroused by the movement of his companion beside him. Arousing himself, he found the fire burning brightly, and saw that the morning was just breaking.

"Awake again?" laughed Johnson. "You seemed to have needed slumber more than I did."

"How long have you been up?"

"Over a half-hour, I guess."

Veghte was out of patience with himself that he should have given this man again the advantage of him, and he arose from his couch in no pleasant mood.

"I can't understand what made me sleep so. If I'd been awake for half a week or so, there might have been some reason."

"You was tired and cold—"

"Johnson, where's that gal?" demanded Basil, suddenly.

"Heaven knows; I don't. When I got up I found she had gone off while we was asleep."

CHAPTER V

> But understand me before a word
> I utter—you do—I knew you must;
> To love a woman like me's absurd.
>
> ROBERT BROWNING.

'WOMEN *is* queer things," was the remark of Basil Veghte, when he had partially recovered from his amazement. "Didn't you see her make off, Johnson?"

"No. I woke about half an hour ago, half froze to death, and got up to throw something on the fire. It wasn't till it got fairly to burning that I noticed she was gone."

"Wal, there's one thing sart'in, she's had to tramp through the snow, and it won't take me long to catch up with her," remarked Veghte, rising, as if to carry his self-suggested idea into execution.

"Man," exclaimed Johnson, "what do you mean? Would you attempt to follow Mariano?"

"Why not?"

"You ought to be shot if you did. What do you suppose she meant by going off as she did? Did she mean you was to follow her and bring her back? If she meant that, what did she go for?"

Veghte scratched his head in perplexity.

"I s'pose that *is* so." Then he added, admiringly, "Johnson, I wish I knowed as much about them critters as you do."

"What critters?"

"Women! There's something about 'em that gits me; they're too much."

"When you get older, you will learn something."

"Older!" responded the woodman. I'm forty-eight years old this very month."

"That's nothing; you haven't seen much of the gentler sex, and it'll take you a good time to learn their ways and manners."

"I'm sure of that."

The two noted, for the first time, that the snow had ceased falling. It already lay in immense depth upon the level, and Veghte could not divest himself of his anxiety regarding the beautiful squaw, whose life he had been the means of saving in such a mysterious manner. He looked out in the snow and discerned her footprints with painful distinctness. The great depth of the snow caused her to move with such difficulty that she left a very irregular trail behind her. He could follow this with his eye for several rods, when the intervening trees—tall, cold, and still—prevented a further view. He did not fail to discover that it led in almost an opposite direction from the spot where he had first discovered her. Whether she had some fixed destination, toward which she was journeying, or whether she had gone off purposely to die by herself alone, could only be determined by conjecture; but, somehow or other, Basil Veghte could not avoid the belief that he had seen the fair Indian for the last time, and that she would never be heard of again.

This thought brought a great sigh, for, out of feelings of humanity, he could but mourn such a sad termination; and the peculiar interest that had been awakened in his heart caused more than one pang in its suppression.

When it was broad day, Johnson remarked:

"If we expect to reach Fort Presq' Isle afore night, it won't do to wait here much longer."

"No; it's going to be a tough piece of work tramping through this snow," remarked Veghte, as he began his simple preparations for departure. "We may calculate upon using ourselves up by night."

"You ain't afeard you can't do it?"

"I've done bigger tramping than this. I'll tell you what would be a good thing for us," remarked Veghte, as if a brilliant idea had just entered his head.

"What's that?"

"Why, to stumble on a pack of red-skins and get 'em started after us. I think we'd make better time tramping than we should without 'em."

"None of us could go very fast."

"I was caught in such a scrape once, and I beat the dogs, though I can tell you it made me work to do it. As we've got to work now, we may as well lay in enough to last all day."

The venison appeared and then disappeared, each eating very heartily. As there was no occasion for their tarrying longer, they set out on their perilous and difficult journey for Fort Presq' Isle. The two had not progressed a mile when it became evident to both that, to reach the station, would compel them to travel during the night, or else to lie over until the next day. Toughened and inured, as they were, to all the hardships of a wilderness life, they found their powers taxed to the utmost to make their way through the snow.

Basil Veghte naturally took the lead, his companion following in his footsteps and experiencing no little difficulty in maintaining an equal pace, notwithstanding his road, in one sense, was "broken" for him. As the former pressed forward, the principal theme of his meditation was regarding Mariano. Was she still alive? Had she perished in the snow? Was she dying at that very moment? Or, had some of her own race found and succored her? Faint, indeed, were the possibilities of the latter being the case.

There was one point that was a source of considerable anxiety to the adventurers. Between them and the fort lay a stream of considerable breadth. As the weather for the last week or two had been comparatively mild, excepting perhaps the last day or two, it was extremely doubtful whether they would find this frozen over sufficiently to allow them to cross upon the ice. If such should be the case, they could only adopt the plan of George Washington and his comrade, who made a similar journey some years before.

It was about noon that this creek was reached. It proved as they had feared all along. For a few feet out from each shore, the stream was frozen over, but in the centre was a space over a hundred feet in width, as free from ice as if it were midsummer. The current here ran very rapidly, which placed the matter in a still worse light, for the case of the illustrious young man just referred to, proved beyond question the exceeding danger of navigating a rapid river in winter by means of a rude raft.

"This is bad," remarked Veghte, after contemplating the open river for a few moments. "That stream must be crossed, if we wish to see Fort Presq' Isle, and how it is to be done is the question."

"Ugh! how will it go to swim it?"

"Can't be thought of; I'd rather walk *around* it, than to go across in that way."

"We must make a raft, then."

Veghte in the mean time was looking up and down stream, as if in quest of something. Johnson observing this inquired what was meant.

"You know the red-men are generally numerous in these parts, and I was thinking that we might stumble on one of their canoes. It would come very handy just now."

"Yes; but how could you manage to see it, when there is such a fall of snow on the ground?"

"They generally turn 'em upside down," replied Veghte, still roaming with his eyes. "And if there should happen to be any such craft layin' loose in that fashion, it would make a sort of hump in the snow, that maybe we might make out. Just take a sharp look, now, Johnson, for I'm mighty anxious to find such a thing, and we haven't a great deal of time on our hands."

Each scrutinized the shores of the creek with patient skill, and finally Johnson detected a swell in the snow to which he called attention. Unfortunately, however, it was on the opposite side, and therefore under the present circumstances could be of no benefit to them. Veghte, in the mean time, was scanning the trees and general contour of the forest, at this particular portion, as if seeking to locate himself. Suddenly his eye brightened.

"I was almost certain, Johnson, we ain't fur from Injins. Last summer I laid in the woods over there, and seen a dozen canoes cross here, again and again. And I've crossed the river in 'em more nor once myself," he chuckled. "Yes, sir, Johnson, if we make a good hunt, we can't help finding 'em."

Veghte was enthusiastic, and immediately began a careful search along the stream. A sudden shout announced success, and looking in that direction, Johnson saw him kicking the snow hither and thither, like one mad. When he reached him, he was in the act of lifting the canoe over his head.

"What do you think of that, Johnson?"

"Very good; you're a lucky man, Veghte."

"Sometimes; ah! here is the paddle. Hello! Injins, by heaven! make for the water. Quick!"

The dull crack of several rifles broke the stillness, and looking in the direction from which they came, our friends saw five Indians tearing through toward them. They needed no stronger inducement to hasten; and although Veghte was impeded with the weight of the canoe, he reached the edge of the stream several feet in advance of his companion.

"Tumble in," he admonished. "They're coming like all creation. Dodge your head! there's a fellow aiming at you."

Johnson dodged his head, and his whole body, though he deserved no credit for so doing, as his excessive fright caused him to tumble headlong into the canoe, coming within a hair's breadth of swamping it.

Catching the long, ashen paddle, Veghte dipped it deep in the water, and drove it swiftly forward with no unskillful hand. By this time, the leaden messengers of the Indians were whistling uncomfortably close around their ears.

"Johnson, this must be stopped!" exclaimed Basil, as he dropped his paddle, and caught up his rifle. "I've been hit, already, and if they blaze away in that fashion, we'll never git over. Hain't you got my gun? Hand it to me."

Johnson attempted to obey, but with so much trepidation that the rifle fell from his hand, and, in spite of Veghte's frantic efforts to prevent it, tumbled overboard and sunk instantly out of sight. The exclamation that fell from the lips of the woodman, at this mishap, we shall not record. He instantly added: "Take your own gun, and see whether you can do anything with that."

The moment Johnson raised his piece, the five savages dropped into the snow, as if they had been shot.

"Keep them there, till we get across!" said Basil; "don't fire as long as they're afeard."

The Indians, however, were not to be kept at bay in this manner. They realized too well the importance of their time to allow the white men to escape. Veghte caught up his paddle again, but the momentary trifling had allowed the canoe to drift several yards down stream, seeing which the Indians arose from the snow, and shouting at the top of their voices, ran rapidly down the bank, firing continually. Johnson raised his gun, whereupon they dodged about so as to distract his aim, not seeking, however, to conceal themselves, as they had just done.

Their situation was now becoming desperate. Veghte was on the point of telling his companion to fire, when the latter did so, his bullet speeding far wide of the mark. By this time the woodman had lost all patience. Throwing his paddle down again, he caught the gun **from his hand**.

"See whether you know enough to manage a paddle. You don't know anything about a gun."

The man rose obediently, and plied the paddle so vigorously that the canoe shot swiftly toward the opposite bank, and was already within a few feet of the ice-bound shore, when one arm and the other hand were struck simultaneously, and he dropped the paddle from his nerveless fingers.

"It's no use, Veghte; I'm good for nothing to-day. It's all up with me."

"Get down in the bottom of the canoe, where they can't hit you. I'll take you over, if they'll give me a minute longer."

The firing at this juncture, from some unaccountable cause, ceased. Perhaps the savages imagined the whites were already secured; for no sooner had Basil Veghte dipped his paddle in the current than three shots were fired, and Johnson, who was not able completely to screen himself, called out that he was struck again. Understanding how inestimably precious was each moment, the woodman plied his paddle with such effect, that, a moment later, the prow grated against the ice-border, and he sprung ashore.

"Come quick!" he called out to his companion, retaining the canoe with his left hand, and reaching forth his right to assist him ashore. Johnson shook his head.

"It's no use, it can't be done."

"What do you mean? Come, Johnson, the rascals will riddle us, if we wait."

"I'm hurt too bad to travel. Take my gun and go; you will need it—I don't."

Veghte looked at him a moment, as if unable to decide what to do.

"Give us your hand, I will help you. Come!"

The last word was fairly shouted, for the danger was too fearfully imminent to admit of this dallying. But Johnson reached forward his gun, and shook his head. Veghte accepted the proffered weapon.

"Good-by, old boy. Keep a good heart. Maybe they won't harm you any more."

With these words, Basil darted away through the snow, first taking the precaution to pull the prow of the canoe upon the ice, so as to give the Indians all the trouble possible before securing the prey that was now absolutely certain. He knew that he was wounded, but he trusted not severely, although, as yet, he had not been given the opportunity to ascertain the extent of his injuries. In the tumult of his emotions, it did not escape his notice, after going a hundred yards, that the firing and shouting upon the part of the Indians entirely ceased. Had he been given the power to observe what transpired behind him, immediately after his departure, he would have experienced more wonder than ever.

Horace Johnson waited until certain his friend was beyond sight, when he rose to the sitting position, and, looking toward the savages, made a signal with his hand. What the particular meaning of this was it would be difficult to tell. If it was meant to check the firing it certainly succeeded, for not another gun was discharged. It may have been a mere token of submission; but, if such, it was certainly curious that the man should shove the canoe free with his own hand, and then take the paddle and commence making his way back toward the shore which he had just left. Curious, we say, principally for the reason that he appeared so badly wounded, when Basil Veghte was in the boat, as to give up all efforts toward propelling it. But our friend saw nothing of these strange movements, and it was well for his peace of mind that he did not.

Veghte had gone, perhaps, a quarter of a mile, when he began to feel as though he had done wrong in deserting his companion as he had done. True, self-preservation demanded such a course, but it seemed that he ought to attempt to rescue Johnson from the hands of his merciless captors.

With these thoughts strong upon him, he paused in his journey, and finally turned to retrace his steps. His experience had taught him to be cautious in his movements, and he approached the creek with great circumspection. When he stood upon the spot where he had bidden his comrade good-by he saw nothing of the canoe or any living person. All had departed.

"I'm afeard Johnson has gone under. I never liked the man much, but I didn't wish him ill. We must all go the same way, sooner or later."

With these reflections, he once more resumed his journey, and late that night reached the wished-for haven, Fort Presq' Isle.

CHAPTER VI.

A life in the woods, boys, is ever as changing;
With proud independence we season our cheer,
And those who the world are for happiness ranging,
Won't find it at all, if they don't find it here.
G. P. MORRIS.

FORT Presq' Isle stood on the southern shore of Lake Erie, near the present site of the town of Erie. At one of its angles was a large block-house, a favourite species of structure on the frontier a century since. It was two stories in height, and strongly built of massive timber, the diameter of the upper story exceeding the lower by several feet, so that the defenders could fire through the openings in the projecting floor upon their assailants below. The roof being covered with shingles, could be easily set on fire; and, conscious of this fearful weakness, an opening was provided at the summit, though which, partially protected by planks, the garrison might dash water upon the flames.

The location of Presq' Isle was most unfortunate. It stood upon a projecting point of land, between the lake and a small brook, which entered it nearly at right angles. Within less than a hundred and fifty feet of the block-house the bank of the brook rose in a high, steep ridge, which offered an effectual screen to an attacking party, while the lake afforded the facilities, upon the other side, of a sudden approach.

The period in which the incidents we are relating are supposed to have occurred, will be recognized as that momentous crisis when the great Pontiac—the renowned chief of the Ottawas—was making the most gigantic efforts to exterminate the English trespassers upon their hunting-grounds, who, since the time of King Phillip, had, year by year, been driving the red-men before them. While the chieftain himself, with a thousand chosen followers, was laying siege to Detroit, the warriors of several tribes, that he had incited to heroic deeds by his burning eloquence, were busy elsewhere. Along the vast frontier were erected forts, garrisoned in too many instances by an inadequate force, whose commanders were lulled into delusive security by the unusual quiet which reigned around them. Separated from each other by hundreds of miles of trackless wilderness, they frequently passed months without hearing tidings of what transpired among their nearest neighbours.

Fort Sandusky fell during the middle of May, 1764. St. Joseph, at the mouth of St. Mary's river, on Lake Michigan, followed a few days later; then Michilimackinac; then Ouataton, on the Wabash, and the Fort Miami, on the Maumee. But as we have chiefly to do with Presq' Isle, we can pause only to glance at those incidents which form some important episodes in our own history.

Late one afternoon in June, Ensign Christie, the commander at Presq' Isle, stood without the block-house, or the edge of the lake, in conversation with Basil Veghte, the hero of the preceding pages. Christie was a muscular iron-limbed man, with a stern face, marked by a determined character, controlled by an intelligent will. He had a rather pleasant voice; and, as he conversed, he stood with his arms folded and his head down, while he varied the conversation by kicking the pebbles with his foot. Veghte as was generally the case, was smoking, and when he wished to gesticulate, invariably took his pipe from his mouth and made his gestures with that in his hand Christie rarely raised his eyes from the ground, except perhaps, when he balanced a stone upon his foot, and then looked out upon the lake to see how far he could cast it while the woodman was glancing in every direction—now upon the placid face of Lake Erie, then at the wood around and behind him—barely sustaining his gaze upon a fixed point for a minute at a time. This restlessness, that was ever observant, was solely the result of his peculiar training. It invariably characterizes the frontiersman.

"Yes," remarked Christie, alluding to what had been previously said by his companion. "I don't think the quietude among the Indians is a good omen. They keep away from the fort, and I began to think, this afternoon, that there weren't so many of 'em in the neighbourhood. It strikes me that they have gone off somewhere."

"They hain't gone fur; you can make up your mind to that. There's enough of the varmints all over, without any of ours going off to join 'em."

"I should like to hear from Detroit," added Christie, after a moment's pause. "There was an Indian through here last week, the day that you were out hunting, who tried to tell us something. All any of us could make out was '*Pontiac Detroit.*' I didn't pay much attention to what he said, but since then I have made up my mind that something has gone wrong, and the savage was trying to tell us about it."

"You don't think that old chief has taken the place?"

"I am afraid so."

"I can't believe it. When I was there, it struck me as being about the safest place a man could stow himself in, if an Indian war should break out."

"That may all be, providing these savages would fight like white men. But, Basil, you and I know well enough what is their fashion of doing things. If they should attack openly, Major Gladwyn might laugh their efforts to scorn; but I'm afraid they've managed to throw him off his guard."

"I know; but hasn't he been in the woods as long as you, and *you* wouldn't be apt to be catched by them."

"My circumstances may have taught me more than his have taught him. Perhaps I should have been deluded by this *false* stillness, if I had not been warned by you."

"Don't know 'bout that. I should be a nateral fool if I hadn't learnt Injin ways by this time."

"You remember that trouble you and Johnson got in

last winter—the night you came in wounded, and nearly frozen to death?"

"I shall not forget that soon."

"Have you seen or heard any thing of Johnson since?"

"No. Poor fellow, when I left him he was about used up. He was hurt pretty bad, and they was so close behind there was no getting out of their way, unless he should have flopped out the of canoe and gone to the bottom rather than fall into their hands."

"It was the same man who visited the fort last summer?"

"Yes; he has been here several times."

"Well, Basil, I saw that man the other day."

Veghte raised his head in amazement. Christie quietly smiled.

"Yes, I saw him, as plainly as I see you this very minute. He was not a hundred yards away."

"Where?"

"Up that very creek. I was out hunting, you remember, on Thursday. I went up this creek about a half-mile, and, happening to come to the water rather suddenly, what should I see but a canoe coming down the stream. I had just sufficient time to step back when it passed, and sitting in the stern was Mr. Horace Johnson, apparently as well as either you or myself."

"Possible! I'm glad to hear it. I thought the man had met his last sickness. I s'pose the Injins have nursed him up and he has managed to give 'em the slip."

"That may be, but if so, one or two slipped away with him. He was in company with two of them, rigged out in their war-paint."

Basil Veghte looked in the face of the commander as if unable to comprehend his meaning.

"One of the savages I knew; the other I never saw to my knowledge. You are acquainted with one also."

"Who do you mean?"

"Balkblalk—that big, rascally-looking Ottawa—that I never fancied, for all he has hung around us for a year or two."

"Johnson is in bad company," replied the woodman. "That Ottawa is a man who would delight to stab you in the dark. I'm sure he fired his rifle at me once, and it was only the goodness of God that saved me. If I had a good excuse, I'd soon put him out of the way."

"Not at present. Let us avoid all cause of offence against the Indians. They're our enemies now, without need of making them more bitter."

"That was a strange adventure, Basil," remarked Christie, after another moment's pause. "Your finding that Indian girl alone in the woods, during that great snow-storm last winter."

"Yes, it has been a great wonder to me ever since. If it had only been a man, I might have got to the bottom of it."

"Why should the fact of a woman, or rather a girl, being in the case make it more difficult?"

"Women is such queer things," he remarked, disconsolately. "I can't tell anything about 'em."

For the next minute or two Ensign Christie employed himself in kicking the pebbles without raising his head. He smiled quietly at the observation of his untutored companion, but said nothing. The latter, however, was busily employed in gazing down the lake shore, as if he had descried something unusual. Suddenly he exclaimed:

"Christie, just take a look down that shore, and tell

me whether there isn't a boat coming. Yes, I know the is."

Christie looked in the direction indicated, and instant answered:

"Yes, there's a boat with a goodly number of men in and they're coming in this direction."

"There are two of 'em," added Veghte. "Do you see on has turned out into the lake, and the other is following Now it's behind it. They've l'arnt enough to keep off th shore."

"They ain't more than a mile off," said Christie. "The are using their oars as though they were pretty tired Notice how slowly they rise and fall."

"No doubt they've been to work all day."

"What can be the meaning of this, Basil?"

"I'm sure I can't tell. May be they've found out tha danger does hang over Presq' Isle, and they've come to lend a hand."

"Worse than that. I'm afraid some post has fallen, and they're the survivors fleeing away."

"What place can it be? Fort Sandusky?"

"Just the fort that was in my mind. There's something wrong; you may rest satisfied regarding that."

By this time some of the men at the block-house had descried the approaching boats, and came out upon the point of land to receive them. Shortly after the boats rounded to, and the men landed. They numbered about forty as jaded and wearied a set of men as could be well imagined. Several arms in slings and bandaged faces showed that they had seen hard usage.

The commander, Lieutenant Cuyler, came directly to Ensign Christie, with the announcement: "I have **bad news** for you."

"I was certain of that," replied the other, waiting anxiously for his communication. While employed in giving it, the men accepted the cordial offer of hospitality, and entered the fort to receive rest and refreshment, and to tell their tale of horror.

"These are all that are left of ninety-six men," said the lieutenant. "We left Fort Niagara on the thirteenth of May, and spent day after day coasting along the northern shore of Lake Erie. We were on our way to Detroit.

"Why were you going there?"

"Haven't you heard that Pontiac has been besieging Detroit for months past?"

"Indeed I had not, although my suspicions were that all was not right with Major Gladwyn."

"Everything is wrong with him. He is sorely pressed, and I fear—very much fear—it will soon be up with him and his garrison."

"Is it as bad as that?"

"A runner reached us with an urgent request for reinforcements and ammunition, and we started as soon as possible. We did not attempt to reach Major Gladwyn, for it would have been sure destruction to have attempted it after our disasters. So we have started to return, and are thus far on our way."

"I am anxious to hear your narrative, lieutenant; but will you not accept refreshment? You appear exhausted."

"It will take but a few moments. After many days we reached Point au Pelée, near the mouth of Detroit river, where we concluded to make a landing. We rowed back and forward, examining the shore to see whether there were any signs of Indians; but we couldn't discover the least evidence of danger—"

"A sure sign that there *was* mischief in the wind," remarked Basil Veghte.

"You may be sure if we had seen any thing suspicious, we should have kept off. We had some seven or eight boats that were drawn up on the beach, while we made our preparations to escape. One of our men and a boy went into the woods to gather some firewood, when an Indian sprung up, tomahawked the boy, and made after the man, who came dashing into camp with the alarm. I formed the men at once into a semicircle around the boats, and told them to be sure and stand firm, as it would be fatal if any of them gave way. It came upon the poor fellows so suddenly that they hadn't time to collect their wits, and I saw the prospects were bad if a determined attack should be made.

"Well, I had hardly got them in order, when the red demons began firing from the woods, and our men returned the fire with spirit. If the Indians had been out where they could have been seen, things might have turned out differently; but, you know how demoralizing it is, ensign, for a body of regular soldiers to fight an unseen foe which is raining a tempest of death into their ranks. The Indians must have seen the fright of our men; for, a few minutes later, the whole body came pouring out of the woods, with their hideous yells that made my blood run cold. I shouted to the men to stand firm; but one sight of the painted redskins was enough. They had hardly reached the centre of the line, when it broke and all made a blind rush for the boats. As might be expected, they threw away their guns, which were caught up by the savages, who kept up the pursuit with an unremitting fierceness.

"Somehow or other, the men managed to get five of the boats afloat, and piling in until they sunk nearly to their gunwales, pushed out from the land. Finding it was all day with us, I waded up to the neck in water and climbed into one of the retreating boats. No one seemed to notice me in the confusion of the moment, or I should have been tomahawked most certainly.

"Well, sir, would you believe it, the Indians shoved out in two of the other boats, overtook the men, and brought three of the boats in to shore again, the soldiers being so frightened that they did not make the least resistance. The other two boats, in which we have just landed, made their escape, and here we are. We rowed all night and the next morning rested awhile on a small island."

"Did you stop at Fort Sandusky?"

"We did; and found it burned to the ground."

"Heavens! is it possible?"

"Yes; that, too, has fallen, and your post will share the same fate."

"You speak confidently, lieutenant."

"What pack of red-skins could resist the temptation to attack you, when you have offered them such inducements? Notice the bank of that creek and the bank of this lake. Could they wish any thing better to insure your destruction?"

"I know that this fort was constructed in a most short-sighted manner that I could never comprehend. But there will be two parties concerned in the destruction, you know."

"That may all be; but it must fall; mark my words for it. It isn't in the power of human beings to prevent it. I don't want to alarm you, but I must tell you what to expect."

"You don't alarm me," smiled Christie. "There are strong arms and brave hearts to defend this to the last."

"I don't doubt it, but it can not avail. That arch-demon, Pontiac, is arousing all the tribes of Indians, and the most terrible of danger now hangs over you. Ensign, I will now accept your kind offer of hospitality."

The three passed within the fort. All was done to make the stay of their visitors as pleasant as it could be under the circumstances. On the morrow they took their departure, and made their way to Niagara, where they reported their loss to the commanding officer.

Before resuming the thread of our narrative, we will give in a paragraph the fate of the three boat-loads of men, of Cuyler's command, that were captured by the Indians. They were taken up to Pontiac's camp, above Detroit, and there massacred in the most revolting manner. "On the following day," says Parkman, in his life of Pontiac, "and for several succeeding days, the garrison at Detroit beheld frightful confirmation of the rumors they had heard. Naked corpses, gashed with knives and scorched with fire, floated down on the pure waters of the Detroit, whose fish came up to nibble at the clotted blood that clung to their ghastly faces!"

CHAPTER VII.

Rude was the garb and strong the frame
Of him who plied his ceaseless toil;
To form that garb, the wild-wood game
Contributed their spoil.—A. B. STREET.

THE visit of Lieutenant Cuyler and his men served the good purpose of warning Ensign Christie and his garrison of the true state of affairs. They realized, for the first time, the extent of that giant conspiracy which Pontiac had set on foot, and the imminent danger which hung over he isolated forest garrisons. These, scattered hundreds of miles apart, could be regularly besieged and reduced until all had fallen. Christie knew that, in the nature of events, the turn of Presq' Isle must speedily come. He should never be so faint-hearted as to surrender, nor so short-sighted as to be taken off his guard by the wily Indians, as too often had been the case along the frontier. He should fight as long as there was a ray of hope; but the disadvantage of the fort's location that had been pointed out to him by the lieutenant had struck him before, and had caused many an hour's anxiety. The savages understood warfare well enough to accept the advantages that had been placed in their way, and under the protection of the two banks they might rain a perfect tempest of bullets without exposing their persons to the least danger in return.

On the day of the departure of Cuyler and his men, Ensign Christie was at the edge of the lake, kicking the pebbles and meditating upon the gloomy future. It was about the middle of the forenoon of one of those magnificent spring days that frequently visit this latitude. At any other time he would have been elated and joyous, but his spirits were now oppressed by a vague and awful fear that was gradually taking shape and spreading its shadows over him.

A footstep caught his ear, and looking up he saw Basil Eghte approaching.

"I don't know whether you want to be disturbed," said the latter, as he came up, and took his pipe from his mouth, "but I've been watching you for the last hour, seein' you holdin' your head down, and knocking the stones about with your feet, by which I knowed there was something troubling you."

"I'm glad to see you, Basil; there is a good deal on my mind. Since Cuyler and his men were here last night I've been thinking upon what they told me. I believe Detroit and all the frontier forts will fall."

"What makes you think so, ensign?"

"The commanders are so foolish as to allow themselves to be blinded by the unnatural stillness of the Indians. Major Gladwyn has probably been aroused in time; but, as he holds the most important post, so Pontiac himself with his selected warriors, is besieging the place. If Cuyler and his men, with their supplies and ammunition, had been able to reach the fort, the major and his garrison might have been saved. But the matter has now a far different aspect."

"Matters do look a little squally, I'll own; but I don't fear for us. Remember, it was rather a dark day, when Presq' Isle was built, and there are enough of us to make a good fight. As for me, I'd kind of like a good brush with the red-skins, it has been so long since I've been in any scrimmage."

"My anxiety is not alone for this fort. What is to become of the English possessions in America, if the frontier posts are to fall, after the fashion of Sandusky? The French, you can understand, are at the bottom of this, and every fort of ours that falls is just so much gain to them; more than so much gain, indeed, for it inspires the Indians with contempt for our power, and respect for that of their 'French Father.'"

For the last moment or two, Veghte had been engaged in looking out upon the lake. The earnestness of his look attracted the attention of Ensign Christie, who inquired:

"Do you see anything suspicious?"

"There's a canoe coming over the lake. We're to have more visitors."

The surface of Lake Erie was unusually still, and the two men descried far out from shore a dark object, that at first look resembled a bird floating upon the water. Closer scrutiny, however, revealed that it was a canoe, slowly heading in toward shore. Shortly after, Basil Veghte announced that it contained two persons.

"Perhaps the survivors of some other post that has fallen. Can it be that they have come from the opposite side?"

"They may have been chased from the shore."

"They will soon be here. Do you observe the flashing of the oars?"

"Yes, the man that handles that knows how to paddle a canoe. Looks to me as if it was a red-skin."

For a few moments both remained silent and motionless, watching the approaching boat. Basil Veghte was the first to speak.

"Yes, an Injin has the paddle, and a white man is sitting in front."

"Who can they be? They look familiar."

An exclamation escaped the woodman. He had recognized both.

"Look close, ensign; can't you make 'em out?"

"I'm sure I can not; although there is some familiarity in the appearance of both. You appear to have identified them."

"I have. Who do you s'pose they are?"

"I can not tell, I am sure."

"S'pose you make a guess."

"It is no use. I shall have to wait until they land, if you do not choose to tell me."

"Well, sir, the man in front is Horace Johnson, and that painted Injin is that old scamp, Balkblalk."

"Is it possible? What can they want with us?"

"We'll soon see, for they're purty close."

Shortly after, the canoe landed at the very feet of the two men, when Horace Johnson sprung ashore and grasped the hand of Basil Veghte. Balkblalk remained behind, dark, sullen and silent.

"You hardly expected to see me, I reckon," remarked Johnson, with a laugh.

"No, nor that painted scamp behind you."

"He's a good fellow. What's the matter with him?"

"Nothing, only he is very full of the devil, and as ugly, too, as a panther."

Johnson laughed, and then turning toward the savage, said:

"You can go, Balkblalk."

One powerful sweep of the paddle sent the canoe back into the water, and the next moment, it went skimming like a bird, straight out on the surface of the lake.

"I'm going to stay with you awhile," added Johnson. "It has been some time since I've visited the fort."

"Haven't you been in the neighbourhood, lately?" asked Christie.

"Yes; I and that red-skin was hunting last week, and we intended to give you a call, but put it off too late."

This declaration was undoubtedly truth, and it somewhat surprised both listeners. There was a cordiality and good-nature in the words and appearance of their visitor, that caused both to wonder somewhat at the ugly suspicions they had entertained.

"When I left you on that day last winter," remarked Basil, "I never expected to see you alive again."

"Nor did I expect to see you. I think it was about the nearest approach to death that I ever made."

"How was it you escaped?"

"I didn't exactly escape; for you know there was no getting away from the Injins, in my condition. I made a sign to them of surrendering, hardly hoping they'd notice; but somehow or other they did. One of them swam over in the icy water, and paddled the canoe to the other shore, when they all got in and went down-stream, till they got to their village, which wasn't fur off, and there took care of me till I got well."

"Didn't you get a chance to run away?"

"I wasn't fit, if I'd been given the chance, till a month or so ago."

"How is it you're free now?"

"I took it into my head to walk away one morning, and done so, and here you see I am."

"How is it you picked up that Injin that is paddling on the lake?"

"I happened to come across him one day, and thought it more wise to be friendly, than to kick up a row with him."

"I s'pose that was the best. Where's the old villain gone now?"

"Off on a hunt, like 'nough. You won't see him again for a month."

"Johnson," said Christie, "do you know any thing of the mishap that has befallen Lieutenant Cuyler and his men?"

"No; what do you mean?"

"He landed near the other end of the lake with nearly a hundred men, and was attacked and lost one half of them."

"Is it possible!" exclaimed his listener, in genuine astonishment. "I hadn't heard a word of it."

"Nor that Detroit is besieged by Pontiac?"

"Never a word. What is getting in the Indians?"

"What has always been in them—the devil," replied the ensign, impatiently, kicking a stone into the lake. "There is going to be hot times in this section, before long."

"I think not," said Johnson, thoughtfully. "There may be a little trouble in different places, as there always is, you know."

"This is something more than usual. I have been fearing it all along, and it is now coming."

"*You* don't fear, do you?" asked Johnson, looking sharply into the face of Christie.

"Fear what? An attack?"

"Yes."

"I do, and that right speedily."

Horace Johnson burst into a loud laugh.

"What cause have you to fear? What stronger fort need you than you have? What braver men need you than your garrison?"

"None; but I wish a better location. But you come to remain with us. It is near noon."

"I can stay only until to-morrow."

Ensign Christie led the way, and the three entered the fort. Johnson was recognized by many of the garrison, who greeted him cordially. He was talkative, and there was a species of dry humor about him that made him good company almost at any time. He was full of anecdote, and served well to while away many an hour that otherwise would have been monotonous and gloomy.

That night, as Basil Veghte had sought his quarters and

was in the act of retiring, Ensign Christie came to him, and, in a whisper, asked him to accompany him to the look-out at the top of the block-house.

"There is something going on that I don't understand. I have been watching it for half an hour."

"What is it?"

"You shall see in a moment."

"Where is Horace Johnson?"

"Gone to sleep. It isn't far from midnight."

"Are you *sure?*" asked Basil. "Have a sharp eye to all his movements."

"There is a man watching him, and he reports that there has been nothing in the least suspicious in his movements. I begin to think, Basil, that we have nothing to fear from him."

"Maybe not, and then again, maybe we have. P'raps we're mistook in our notion, but I can't think so yet."

A few moments later the two men were at the top of the block-house. Christie addressed the man who was stationed there:

"Where is it, Jim?"

"It has gone, sir—no, there it is."

Out upon the surface of Lake Erie appeared a point of light that resembled a star floating upon the water. A casual glance would have pronounced it such; but there was an unsteadiness about it—a moving to and fro—that identified it beyond dispute.

"How long has it been there, Jim?" inquired Veghte.

"I first noticed it about half an hour ago, which isn't a sign it hasn't been there longer. I wasn't thinking of looking *there* for any thing, or I might have seen it the minute it come. What might you take it to be, sir?" inquired the man, with considerable curiosity.

3

"It's mighty hard to tell—not so hard either. It's some Injin contrivance; you may make up your mind to that."

"But would an Indian show a light in that manner, when they might be sure we'd see it?" inquired Christie.

"Maybe they want it to be seen."

"Hold!" exclaimed the commander, in an excited tone. "They may be the remnants of some garrison—perhaps Sandusky—and they're afraid to land for fear the Indians have Presq' Isle."

"No, I don't think it can be that. They could send a man ashore who would soon find out."

"What *can* it mean, then?"

"Maybe a lot of French and Injins that have got some of their treacherous rascals in this fort, and are making signs to them. Don't you know of such a one?"

"We haven't any here," said Christie, confidently. "All are good and true men. Are they not, Jim?"

The man coughed and hesitated, and made no reply. The commander was about to press him further, when Basil spoke in a low voice:

"Ensign, just watch that light. It is moving up and down. I am going out in a canoe to see what it is."

"You'll run great risk, Basil; but you can take care of yourself, I suppose."

"I think so."

The woodman was a man of few words when it was necessary to act. He made his way out of the fort, and, without any one accompanying him, reached the shore of the lake. A moment later he shoved out in his ever-ready canoe, and began his noiseless and perilous journey.

As he rowed away, he glanced back at the shore, and

discovered the outlines of a man of gigantic stature, apparently watching him.

"Is that you, ensign?" he asked, in a cautious undertone.

"Yes. Hurry back."

It was a stranger's voice, and Basil Veghte was not deceived. He chose to appear so. "All right!" he replied, and then he asked himself, as he went out in the darkness: "Who can that big man be? I never heard his voice before, and there's nobody in the fort that looks like him."

CHAPTER VIII.

Humble the lot, yet his the race,
When Liberty sent forth her cry,
Who thronged in conflict's deadliest place,
To fight—to bleed—to die.—A. B. STREET.

No man realized that his journey was a perilous one more than Basil Veghte realized that he had ventured upon an exceedingly delicate and dangerous undertaking. That there were enemies upon the surface of Lake Erie, in close proximity to Presq' Isle, there could be no doubt. Whether they were French or Indians, or both, what their number was, and their intentions, he had taken upon himself to determine so far as it was possible for a man to determine.

Fortunately the lake was still; that is, comparatively so. The water of the great lakes being fresh, is more easily disturbed than the ocean by the passing wind, and rarely is the surface perfectly unruffled. We have dwelt years upon the southern shore of Erie, and have never yet seen it *perfectly* calm. Basil Veghte was scarcely clear of the shore, when he held his paddle suspended and listened. Not a sound, save the sullen roar of the lake, reached his ears. Then he leaned forward, and, with his eagle eye, endeavored to pierce the Stygian darkness; but all was blank as chaos itself.

A faint wavering call, such as a bird sometimes makes to its mate, reached his ears.

"That's no bird," he reflected. "That came from the shore, and that big fellow made it. It isn't intended for me, but I'll take the benefit."

Fully ten minutes elapsed, when precisely the same sound was repeated. The wily woodman comprehended it at once, and quietly smiled.

"He ain't sure they heard it, and it is meant to give 'em warning that Fort Presq' Isle has smelt their mischief. He won't make that sound again. I'm sorry he seen me, for I might've stole on 'em without their s'picioning it, and now they'll be on the look-out."

Veghte was right, for, although he carefully listened, the sound was not repeated. The man who had given the signal evidently took it for granted that its second utterance could not fail of a proper audience.

Could the darkness that rested on the bosom of Lake Erie on that spring night, in 1764, have been swept away, it would have revealed a picture worthy the pencil of an artist. A small canoe, almost motionless upon the water—in the centre the iron-limbed woodman, his rifle resting in his lap, his long paddle, held in both hands, barely inserted a few inches in the water—toying, idling, just moving the frail vessel, so that there might be no inconvenient impetus to overcome, if a sudden emergency should call for a lightning-like retreat—the rigid form of the man, so rigid that the almost imperceptible dallying of the paddle seemed born of itself—a sort of fin-like quivering of its extremity, the head turning constantly in every direction, the dark eyes seeming fairly to flash fire in their persistent search into the black void. These were the salient points of the picture. There were other accompaniments, perhaps still more interesting, but these were yet to be discovered.

Fully a half-hour elapsed before the strained eye and ear of Veghte detected any thing suspicious. Then a slight ripple in the water, followed by a momentary flash of light. This appeared directly behind him, proving that he had passed the object of his search. Consequently, when returning, he ran a risk of colliding with the suspicious craft, unless extreme care were used.

By this time, Basil concluded that there was only one boat besides his own canoe, cruising along the shore. This contained enemies who doubtless were making signals to the fort—signals that as yet had elicited no response. While dallying around in the water, the woodman was conjecturing who the traitor or traitors within Presq' Isle could be. Suspicion naturally fixed upon Johnson, but something seemed to tell him that he was not the man— that there were those in confidence with Ensign Christie, who needed to be feared and watched. He recalled the hesitancy of the sentinel "Jim," when questioned by the commander. He endeavored to decide upon the man, and finally had selected a small, nervous Swede, as the one whose manner invited doubt, when—a bright light was seen to wave to and fro, apparently from the lookout upon the block-house—the very spot where he had stood with Ensign Christie and the sentinel!

Veghte was dumbfounded—to speak literally—at this demonstration. What opportunity could a man have to make a direct reply to the signals of the enemy as had been done before his eyes that very minute? The light disappeared as suddenly as if plunged into the lake, and was seen no more.

A grunt as of satisfaction, recalled the woodman to his situation, and glancing hastily beside him, he was just able to discern a dark shadow resting upon the water—a shadow that he concluded was the canoe he was seeking, not from any evidence of his own vision, but from what he had already seen and heard.

Bending forward, so as to render himself less liable to observation, he noiselessly advanced the canoe a yard or two, and then peered over the gunwale. This glance revealed the fact that the enemies' canoe was motionless, and he now heard them speak to each other, in low tones. His experienced ear told him that he was listening to the words of Indians instead of white men. Basil Veghte would have given his right arm, almost, had he been able to understand the tongue; but he did not, and his eavesdropping could therefore avail him nothing, so long as the words uttered were in that unknown vernacular. A thrill shot through him as he recognized the French language, spoken beyond question. The meaning of the first sentence he was unable to catch, but the second was distinctly understood.

"Too bad! The Yengese are on the watch. They have found us out."

"We can't attack to-night," remarked a second, in the same tongue.

"No; we are not enough, and they are too well prepared."

"The signal was delayed; he must have failed to see us till now."

Basil gave his paddle the slightest possible motion; for he was certain he should hear the name of the traitor pronounced. On the contrary:

"Pierre, isn't that a boat off there in the darkness?"

"It's *something*; hello, there! ahoy!"

One dextrous turn of the paddle, and the canoe shot backward full twenty feet.

"Give 'em a shot! hang him! it's that infernal Yengese, watching us."

The crack of three rifles followed this announcement, and Veghte smiled grimly as the bullets whistled over his head.

"There's another man who occasionally attempts that kind of business, and his name is Basil Veghte, and his rifle's name is Sweetlove, and that's the way she talks, now and then."

Whether his shot took effect he never knew, but he instantly became aware that it was a most imprudent action. The flash revealed his exact location, and the skilled and powerful arms of the Indians sent their own boat after him with exceeding velocity. There was no time to think of firing, as he dropped his piece in the bottom of the canoe, and with a tremendous sweep of his oar, drove his canoe several rods in a direction at right angles to the one he had first pursued. The darkness favored him, and by operating in his noiseless manner, he right speedily secured his own safety.

Fearing that the contingency might arise when he should be compelled to take to the water to escape his foes, he fastened his rifle to his back, so that it could be no incumbrance, and then resumed his reconnoitering. His great object now was to obtain the name of the traitor within the fort; that secured, he deemed Presq' Isle safe from all enemies.

The noise of the receding paddles was plainly heard, and he chuckled to himself as he listened:

"They haven't catched Basil Veghte yet, and they may navigate a considerable while in *that* direction, afore they get scent again."

He now directed his boat after them, so that the scene presented the anomaly of the pursuers being pursued by the pursued, a state of affairs exceedingly interesting to the latter, but not likely to result in any thing important to the former.

"I thought women was the queerest things in natur'," mused Veght, "but here them scamps are after me, and I'm after them, and 'tain't likely one'll catch the other, nor the other catch one, nor both catch neither, nor neither catch both; and that fix is as queer as women."

It required but a few moments for the larger canoe to ascertain that the smaller had escaped beyond the hope of recovery. Its masters therefore gave over their efforts. The chase—if the momentary rivalry can be dignified with the name—taught the woodman a truth that rendered him slightly uneasy. Should the Indians obtain a fair view of him, they could overtake his boat without doubt. Although possessing remarkable skill, he was no match for these warriors, who had probably spent years in the canoe, and learned its management to perfection. He had counted with considerable confidence upon his ability to hold his own, at least, and if he preserved that, he could feel assured of his ultimate escape. But the opposite being the case, his position became doubly perilous.

The circumstances being thus, he debated whether his best plan was not to return to the shore at once, with the information he had obtained. He had learned the probable number of the French and Indians; he had ascertained that they were coasting along the shore to discover whether Presq' Isle was on its guard or not. Its indefatigable commandant being fully on the alert, and they being notified of it, there could be no immediate danger impending over the Forest Garrison, and its brave defenders. The sagacity of Ensign Christie and some of his confidential friends ought to be sufficient to ferret out him or them whose hearts were full only of treachery. That some such a one was in the fort, Basil Veghte considered settled beyond all question. Why then delay his return?

Sober second thought prevailed, and the woodman dipped his paddle into the water with the intention of going ashore, when he detected the hostile canoe silently crossing his prow, so close that every form it contained was clearly outlined in the darkness.

At first Veghte hoped he was not seen, and he leaned his head forward and downward, that his person at least might be invisible. An exultant exclamation and the sudden sweep of paddles undeceived him. So confident seemed the pursuers of their prey, that they did not discharge a gun, when they could have laid the woodman low in an instant.

Now that the actual contest had come, Veghte resolved to do the best he could toward escaping without resorting to the stratagem which he had decided to adopt only at the last extremity. Plying his paddle, therefore, with all the strength and skill at his command, he sent his canoe rapidly forward, and then, as before, turned it off at a sharp angle, hoping that this temporary advantage would shelter him again. The French and Indians were too close, however, to allow the success of this maneuver. While the woodman's canoe described the two sides of a triangle, theirs described the hypothenuse, and thus had their speed been relatively the same, they would have gained an actual advantage. As it was, they came so close, that he discerned the features of a white man and an Indian in the prow of the canoe.

A sudden feeling of terror lent an unnatural strength to the woodman's arm for a moment, and he drove his boat ahead with a velocity that gave him a yard or two the advantage.

"Surrender, you fool!" called out the white man. "We have got you, and stop before I shoot! Do you hear? Surrender!"

Veghte saw the rifle raised in a threatening manner, and he lowered his head, although certain they would not fire, so long as there was a prospect of capturing him. He had an object, however, in the movement, beyond that of feigning the fear he did feel.

"Surrender, I say, you American fool, or I'll stop your rowing?"

"Well, put your gun down, then!" called out the fugitive.

The desperate strait in which Basil Veghte now found himself, caused him to do something that ordinarily is not considered a part of honourable warfare. On the frontier, however, his conduct would have been sanctioned by almost any one, even by those who were the most directly concerned.

Believing he had actually surrendered, the pursuers ceased their strenuous efforts, as their canoe had sufficient momentum to bring it beside the small one. They had scarcely paused, when Veghte impelled his own forward with all the sudden celerity he was capable of using, and, at the moment he was at the furthest point attainable, quietly whisked over the side of the boat into the water.

The advantage gained by this questionable proceeding, (that is, by deceiving his enemies regarding his submission,) was only temporary. It was instantly detected, and taking lesson from the deceit practised upon them, the large canoe was driven over the water without intermission, until its prow touched the side of the smaller one. The last few yards they advanced rather cautiously, as they knew they had a dangerous foe, especially if driven to bay. They fully expected a shot from him, when he should see that all escape was cut off. His head being invisible, they supposed he had leaned forward as before, to escape their shots. A glance of the white man revealed his absence.

"He has gone! He is not in the canoe! Where is he?"

All looked around, to see whether his head was visible, and all listened to catch some sound of his swimming through the water. Nothing was seen nor heard, and they very reluctantly and ill-naturedly came to the belief that they had been outwitted.

The fugitive could be at no great distance, and they described a large circle in the water, hoping they might come upon him. This was continued some time, when they gave up the pursuit altogether.

Upon going into the water, Basil Veghte, as he afterward expressed it, "took a mighty big dive," going down to such a depth that his feet touched the sandy bottom. As fortune would have it, he came up directly behind the Indian canoe, so close that he could have touched the stern by stretching out his hand. Persons accustomed to danger sometimes experience an ecstatic thrill in the moment of extreme peril, and Basil reached his hand up to catch the stern. Fortunately, its swift motion prevented, and he was speedily left behind. Turning squarely around he swam with all his might for shore. The deliberation with which the savages approached his canoe, gave him considerable time, and yet he was just safely beyond the outermost edge of the circle first described by them in their search.

Thinking the canoe might cruise along the shore in the expectation that he would attempt to land, or that the stranger he had seen would be on the look-out for him, Veghte went up the lake several hundred yards, and then cautiously approached the land. When its dim outlines became visible, he eagerly scanned the bank, but could detect nothing suspicious, and thereupon continued his approach.

His feet had just touched bottom, when a figure came out of the darkness, and he recognized the gigantic form that had bidden him farewell upon his departure in the canoe. The man walked down to the edge of the water and gazed out upon the lake as if expecting to see something or some one.

At first, Veghte supposed he had been seen, and he checked his progress; but, the next moment he perceived his mistake, and accordingly continued his course along the lake, until far beyond sight of the man, when he again made his way toward the bank.

CHAPTER IX.

THE WOODMAN A PRISONER.

' Thus doth the ever-changing course of things,
   Run a perpetual circle, ever-turning,
And that same day that highest glory brings,
   Brings us unto the point of back returning."

It was not often that Basil Veghte's eyes deceived him, but they did on this occasion. He had just stepped upon the shingle, and had turned to look out upon the lake, when a hand patted him lightly on the shoulder.

" You are my prisoner, Basil Veghte!"

" There're various 'pinions about that!" exclaimed the woodman, wheeling in his tracks with the intention of disputing this declaration in rather an emphatic manner. But, at that instant, he was seized with a grip of iron from behind, and immovably pinioned.

"It's no use!" exclaimed the first individual, whom Veghte recognized as the large man who hailed him as he shoved out from shore. " You're a prisoner this time, and the best thing you can do is to own up like a man."

While these words were being uttered, the man behind, who possessed prodigious strength, lifted the woodman from his feet, carrying him a short distance, and quietly depositing him in the stern of a canoe that had not caught Veghte's eye. It was then shoved into deep water by the large man, while his comrade seated himself in the middle, and took the paddle. Forcing it out into the water until it was clear of the sand, the large man took his seat in the end of the canoe, so that he sat face to face with the two other occupants. Drawing his cloak around him, Veghte plainly heard the clink of a pistol and saw the huge barrel protrude from his coat.

"The slightest movement, my friend, and your precious body will receive the contents of this. It won't be the first time it has done such a duty."

This was surely a strange position for the scout. The hero of a hundred hair-breadth escapes caught in such a predicament as this! and that, too, after the skillful manner in which he had eluded the French and savages in the water. Well might he reproach himself for his recklessness in exposing himself to such danger.

The accent of his captor betrayed that he was a Frenchman, but his companion was as silent as if he possessed not the power of speech. In spite of the trying circumstances of his situation, the woodman could but admire the magnificent physical development of his sentinel, and the wonderful activity and strength displayed by the oarsman. There was not a man in a thousand who was a match for Basil in these respects; and yet, when seized, he found himself perfectly helpless. True, he was taken at disadvantage, when pinioned in the grip of his adversary; but he was not prevented from calling into play an amount of force that would have told upon almost any thing. He recollected hearing the man pant as though it cost him great effort, but never once did his vice-like grip loosen.

The natural questions the woodman propounded to himself were: What is to be the result of this? Where am I to be taken? What special object am I to call forth these strenuous efforts to capture me?

The services that Veghte had rendered in the French War, were enough distinctly to individualize him among the many heroes of that sanguinary contest; and the subsequent good rendered by him to the English forts along the frontier was sufficient to make him a special target for the Indians.

But the more he reflected upon it, the more did it seem to him as though one of the particular objects of that night's work, upon the part of the French and Indians, had been to secure his person. The maneuvers of those in the large canoe might have been naturally caused by the hope of taking their enemy; but his captor, the large man—appeared to come solely for that purpose. Having now accomplished his desire, they had launched forth in the canoe at once, as if unconscious that they had allies upon the lake.

The woodman was discreet enough to keep his eyes about him, and to improve his advantages so far as it was possible to do so under the circumstances. He observed that the oarsman did not put directly out for the middle of the lake, but took a western direction, along the shore. So close, indeed, were they to the land, that more than once he caught the outline of the woods or some prominent objects familiar for years to his gaze.

It is but just to say that Basil's greatest anxiety was for Ensign Christie and the brave garrison he had left behind him. It can not be said that his own situation did not give him concern; but he had a simple faith in the beneficent Providence that had never forgotten him, and he believed he should ultimately be delivered from the net that had closed around him. Exactly how or when, he could not divine, but was certain the moment of deliverance would come in good season.

But a dark cloud was settling over Presq' Isle. The storm had marshaled its fury, and it was ready to break forth, and he, at the very juncture he was so sadly needed, must be cruelly withdrawn. He upon whom the ensign relied to read the almost invisible signs that were ominous to him and his gallant followers—he who at that moment was watching and waiting for his return—must lose his services.

Ah! was not that the very reason that such determined efforts had been made to capture him?

The question flashed across the woodman's mind like lightning, and with the question and its invariable answer, came the conviction that Mr. Horace Johnson had specially maneuvered for that purpose. The display of signals on the lake had been intended to catch the eye of the sleepless sentinels, and to draw forth the only one of their number who would risk such a perilous attempt. The huge Frenchman and his comrade had been watching along the shore for the purpose of seizing him. Prudence had, doubtless, led them to allow his unmolested departure; but they had taken care that such should not be his return.

All was plain now to the prisoner—the whole plan by which he had been so cleverly entrapped, at the very moment when upon the threshold of safety. At that particular moment, it would have been exceedingly dangerous for Mr. Horace Johnson to have come within reach of Basil Veghte.

It would be idle to say that no thought of escape entered our hero's mind. Scarcely a moment passed that he did not mentally canvass the prospects of giving his captors the slip. He looked sideways at the water which came up to the very gunwales of the canoe, and meditated springing overboard and making a "long dive" for it, as he did when closely pressed by the French and Indians. But there sat his master, with his pistol cocked and pointed, so that it needed but a pressure of the finger to end his career forever. He was well aware that, if the occasion arose, the man would not hesitate a moment either. Not once did he remove his gaze from him, and he seemed to divine the very thoughts that were passing through his mind.

But one stratagem afforded a ray of hope. If he could divert, if but for a moment, the attention of the relentless captor, he might throw himself beyond his reach, and, by skillful diving, finally elude him. This was a desperate resort indeed, but it was the only one that occurred to him, or that could occur only so long as it was night and they were abroad upon the lake.

Before attempting his artifice, Basil waited in the hope that this terrible vigilance would cease or abate. Without allowing it to appear suspicious, he kept his eye fixed upon the Frenchman, waiting only for the second when he should turn his head or lower his weapon. He hoped that the two comrades might exchange places, but it appeared as if the man who held the paddle would never tire, nor did the other show the least manifestation of change. He might as well hoped for an image of iron to change its position as to hope for the turning of that head or the lowering of that muzzle.

Finally the woodman lost all hope in that direction, and determined to bring matters to an issue at once. Had it not been for the unfortunate wetting of his powder, he might have called his own pistols into play. But, for some time to come, they could be of no use whatever.

As if to favor the design of Veghte, a plashing at that moment was heard upon the shore, as though some person or animal had stepped into the water.

"What's that?" he demanded, suddenly turning his head in an alarmed manner.

"No you don't," returned his grim captor, without stirring a hair's breadth. "You can't do any thing that way."

"What way?" asked Basil, in a gruff tone, for he was in no fine humor over the failure of his cherished plan. The large man laughed.

"I understand you, my friend. You are not to blame for wanting to get off, but it can't be done. *You're wanted in another place for a few days!*"

There was a significance in the manner in which the last sentence was uttered that gave it a far deeper meaning than the words themselves would have conveyed. As there seemed to be a species of grim humor in the fellow, Veghte concluded that something might be obtained from him in the course of a conversation.

"What did you want me for?"

A contemptuous laugh greeted this question, which there is no denying was rather foolish.

"What did I want you, for? That's a sensible question to ask! Why does one nation take prisoners of another during war? We took you because we wanted you."

"Just so; what I s'posed; wasn't sart'in, though. Didn't you *want me a little more than you did any one else?*"

The man now laughed heartily.

"You are asking curious questions. I suppose you know as well as every one else that your services for the English have made you quite notorious. You were rather conspicuous in the war, too. Pity you didn't fight on the right side."

"I did; that's the trouble."

"We won't dispute on that point, for it can't be of any use. I s'pose you would have liked to get one of our Generals, wouldn't you? that is, if you were able—"

"But I don't happen to be a General."

"No one said you was; but I rather suspect you have done your side about as much good as any of your Generals. Consequently it will do us considerable good to deprive your friends of your labors *for the present!*"

Again that peculiar meaning tone. The woodman looked at him a moment, and then said:

"You might as well own up, you intend to attack Presq' Isle."

"Who does?"

"You Frenchmen and the Indians, for you work together."

"You are mistaken. You English have done all you could to undermine us ever since this country was discovered. This war is now the work of Pontiac, the great Ottawa chief."

It was Veghte's turn to indulge in a scornful laugh.

"That old heathen knows how to make war—that's true enough—but he couldn't do half if it wasn't for you Frenchmen."

The man addressed made no reply, being, seemingly, too chivalrous to quarrel with one who was in his power. After waiting a proper time, Veghte continued:

"The Injins intend to attack Presq' Isle, don't they?"

"Shouldn't wonder if they did. Things do look rather that way just now."

"I only hope I may be there to riddle a few of the dogs."

"Ha! ha! That's just why we brought you away. There'll not be half the trouble with you gone, that there would be if you remained. You ought to take it as quite a compliment—this making away with you."

"What are all the red-skins doing out on the lake to-night?"

The silence of the Frenchman assured Basil Veghte that he was presuming rather too much on his situation. Nothing daunted, however, he renewed his attack.

"Isn't that Horace Johnson mixed up in this affair?"

"You are asking questions which I can not answer."

"You've answered enough by not making any answer at all. I might have knowed that he and Balkblalk being together meant something uncommon."

Never once, during this conversation, did the captor remove his pointed weapon. Like the finger of fate, it was directed straight at the head of the woodman, who could have drawn out its deadly contents by a single movement of his body.

And never once did the man in the middle of the canoe cease plying his paddle. The conversation appeared to be devoid of all interest to him, and Veghte half suspected he was unable to comprehend English, or was deaf and dumb altogether.

Perhaps the restless, flitting movements of our hero's head warned the Frenchman he was meditating some attempt at escape, and kept him on a constant guard. The former, for the present, could see no ray of hope. Powerful and agile as he was, he could not throw himself out of the canoe with sufficient celerity to avoid the pistol-ball; nor could he reach the water, was it barely possible to make a dive of sufficient skill to avoid the canoe altogether.

Meantime, the quiet, swift progress continued. The same distance from the shore was preserved, for, at short intervals, the dim outlines of the woods could be perceived, and, occasionally, the flash of the waves upon the sand. The prisoner, who had given over his efforts at a conversation for the present, fell to speculating upon his destination. He had skirted the southern shore of Lake Erie from Presq' Isle to Detroit, and he could recall no post where they would likely land. He concluded, therefore, that there must be a war-party encamped somewhere along the lake, whither his captors were carrying him.

It had not escaped the attention of Basil that, for the last ten or fifteen minutes, the wind had been rising, and there was every appearance of a coming "blow." The increasing waves could be heard upon the shore—the dip of the paddle and the unsteady motion of the canoe showed that the surface of the fickle lake was becoming agitated, and that it would soon be aroused to fury.

The woodman rather welcomed this prospect of a change. Deeply laden, as was the canoe, a slight increase of the angry waves would either send it to the shore or the bottom. In case it went to the bottom, it would be just the opportunity he so ardently desired. There could be no fear then but that he would attend to his own safety. In case the canoe put in to land, his escape, although not absolutely assured, would be rendered extremely probable.

The Frenchman evidently intended to keep upon the lake as long as possible, for, notwithstanding the increasing waves and the occasional dashing of the spray into the boat, the oarsman shot straight ahead, and his leader sat with his pistol still pointed at the breast of his captive. True, at every dip of the paddle the body of the silent man interposed as a shield; but, as the lowering of his head constantly brought that of our hero into view, and as the woodman could not change his position without bringing himself in direct range, the presence of the third man made little or no difference.

As it was the wish of Basil Veghte that the canoe should remain out upon the lake, he concluded that the best way to induce his captor to remain there was to express an anxiety to go ashore.

"The lake is gettin' rather rough, and it'll soon be ticklish business to keep afloat."

"There's no danger—a good man has hold of the paddle."

"I see; but it'll take a great deal better man than him to paddle us through, if the waves get much higher. You'd better take my advice and go ashore."

The Frenchman indulged in one of his sarcastic laughs.

"No use, my friend. I understand why you wish to go ashore. You might as well give up your ideas. I understand them too well."

Basil Veghte entertained a strong suspicion that just then he was very far from being understood.

"Do as you please. It don't make any difference to me, I s'pose."

"I think it does—considerable."

"I b'lieve I can manage a canoe as well as you or your friend, and I know *I* couldn't keep the thing afloat, loaded as this is."

"Think as you please—oh!"

The exclamation was caused by a pailful of water dropping in the lap of the speaker. It seemed to disconcert him for a moment, but he was too wily to give his captive any advantage. He addressed his comrade in a low tone, using his own language, which was incomprehensible to Veghte. The latter, however, rightly suspected it was an admonition to be careful in the management of the canoe.

The truth was the frail concern was taken at disadvantage. To breast the waves it was necessary to turn its prow directly out from shore—a proceeding that, besides checking its direction, would give it a course which the Frenchman had every reason for wishing to avoid. Turned broadside to the lake, the canoe was really in imminent danger of filling.

It is not to be supposed that the Frenchman was insensible of the peril in which he was placed, and which was momentarily increasing. While he was well aware of the additional prospects of escape that would be given his prisoner, in case they effected a landing, he had still a stronger reason for keeping on the lake—a reason which was not even suspected by the woodman. It was not long before the latter comprehended it.

Some fifteen minutes after the last exchange of words, Basil detected the soft rush of water, evidence that they were approaching the mouth of a stream which put into the lake. The agitation of the water also proved that they were in its eddy. A moment later a powerful sweep of the paddle brought the canoe at right angles, and, in a few seconds more, the trio were out of Lake Erie, and gliding up the stream.

This stream was partially familiar to the woodman, and a moment's reflection satisfied him that the crisis in his fate was close at hand. Provided the destination was a considerable distance up the creek, there was strong prospect of something "turning up;" but if the Indian encampment (as our hero was certain was their destination) was close at hand, the chances were more desperate than ever.

Something less than a mile from its mouth the stream

became very narrow, and was overhung by dense shrubbery, which, at this season of the year, was almost impenetrable. Basil resolved that if this portion was penetrated by the canoe, he would precipitate matters right speedily.

"How fur do you intend to go up?" he inquired, shortly after they had left the lake.

The Frenchman indulged in a laugh before he replied:

"You are very inquisitive to-night. Why do you want to know?"

"It seems to me you ax about as many questions as I do. I ain't pertick'ler whether you answer or not. I thought it would go a little more pleasant to talk than to keep still."

"I shall be glad to keep up a conversation, but I can't promise to answer every question you ask. However, I'll promise to do so," he added, after a moment's silence, "if you'll answer mine."

"Don't know about that," replied Veghte, with commendable prudence. "I must first hear what your questions might be."

The Frenchman laughed and hesitated some time before speaking, but finally said:

"How many men are in Fort Presq' Isle?"

"You'll find out mighty soon when you attack it."

"I've no doubt, if they are such characters as you. You are hardly willing to tell, I see. Suppose I should say that if you didn't give me a correct answer, I should discharge this pistol. What then?"

"Blaze away!"

"No, sir. The French do not make war in that manner. I demand nothing of you that you are unwilling to give. You might as well afford the information, however, as

Ensign Christie will very soon find those quarters too hot to hold him."

"You and Horace Johnson may think so; but the thing must be tried afore you can tell."

"Exactly. It will not be long, then, before we learn. In fact," added the Frenchman, exultingly, "I think we know now near enough for all practical purposes."

"Johnson is in Fort Presq' Isle this minute. I only hope Christie will keep him there a while."

"You do that man wrong by suspecting him. He is not the bad man you take him to be."

The woodman looked upon this as a weak attempt to throw him off the true scent, and he mentally concluded he should not be deceived. Suspicion, with him, had resolved itself into a certainty regarding the singular actions of this man.

"We must be several miles from the fort," remarked Basil.

"Yes," was the dubious reply.

"You camp at a safe distance. Strikes me you're afraid of being seen."

"Yes; perhaps so, and again perhaps not."

"Do you know how Pontiac is getting along at Detroit?"

"He's doing well. He'll soon bring Gladwyn to terms. That red-skin is a great General."

"I never thought so," returned the woodman, who, like all uneducated persons, found it difficult to see merit in an enemy.

"The fall of all the posts along the lake, I suspect, may be credited to him."

"All the posts haven't fell," was the sturdy rejoinder of our hero; "nor you needn't be sart'in of their falling."

During this conversation Veghte kept a sharp eye about him. He observed, with a thrill of delight, that they were entering upon that extremely narrow passage of the creek—so strait, in fact, that a man in a canoe could touch either shore with his paddle. He observed, too, that his captor manifested considerable uneasiness, as if conscious that affairs were taking a dubious aspect.

The woodman maintained a rambling conversation, not worthy of record, in order to lull the suspicion of the Frenchman. It was not long before they glided beneath a heavy, overhanging mass of limbs, the leaves and twigs of which switched their faces. While passing beneath this, the wily Frenchman felt a sudden shock and lightening of the canoe, and the next moment, when they emerged into more open water, his quick glance revealed the fact that the boat held but two persons! With a furious exclamation, he ordered his comrade instantly to "back water," and, holding his pistol in readiness to fire, peered through the darkness in quest of the head of the daring woodman.

CHAPTER X.

A MYSTERIOUS PURSUER.

"The deep booms smite the trembling air;
Each throb proclaims the foeman near."

THE Frenchman leaned forward and peered through the darkness, expecting each moment to catch sight of the woodman's head, fully resolved, the moment he did so, to send a pistol-ball through it. Around and around the canoe darted, like some wounded and bewildered bird, its movements consorting well with the anxious, restless manner of its inmates, now that they were fully aroused. But, although both used their eyes with all human skill, they saw nothing of Basil Veghte, for the very good reason that neither looked in the proper place.

The woodman's action, although sudden, was carefully deliberated and executed with consummate coolness and dexterity. At the moment the canoe swept under the overhanging foliage, he arose to his feet, and, grasping a strong limb by both hands, quickly lifted himself upward, and glided noiselessly along the stout branch until he reached the old trunk. Around this he whisked to the opposite side, and there crouched, like a wild animal at bay, secure in the heavy foliage.

The situation of the woodman was such that he could see nothing of the Frenchman, although every slightest movement was revealed to his ear. He felt assured of his own escape; but, as there was no occasion to draw his enemy's well-aimed fire, he chose to remain where he was until all danger was gone.

It was natural that Veghte should chuckle to himself, as he heard the muttered execration of the Frenchman, after their fruitless search, and finally heard them commence descending the stream.

"Here's as rather thinks you'll have time to case that arm a little that you kept p'inted at my head so long," he exclaimed, mentally, as he saw their relinquishment of the search.

He now descended from his perch, and paused a moment to locate himself. There was little difficulty in this, as their course from the beginning had been understood. It occasioned him considerable wonder that the two men should descend the creek. Beyond question, they must have had some definite destination, toward which they had been carrying him, and now that he had been lost to them, they had given over their journey, and most probably were returning to the great centre of interest—Presq' Isle.

As the woodman stood debating with himself, a cold sweat broke out upon him at a terrible suspicion that suddenly came to his mind. It was now clear why they wished to make their way up this lonely creek. It was for no other purpose than to murder him!

The storm which seemed rapidly approaching, began suddenly to die away, and, as is often the case along Lake Erie, soon subsided entirely, and the waves of the lake returned to their usual undulating swell. The storm had burst over the inland sea, and was far away toward the beleaguered town of Detroit.

As Veghte moved away from the dense shrubbery, he caught the outlines of the canoe slowly and almost silently descending the stream. He could just make out the forms of the two men in the darkness. While looking at them he stepped upon a branch that broke with a sharp crackle. He noticed that the paddling instantly ceased, and the men were evidently listening.

"Hello!" finally called the large Frenchman.

"Wal, hello! What of it?"

"Is that you?"

"I kinder s'pect it is."

"How came you to give us the slip?"

"Ha! ha! I just stepped out to stretch my legs."

Basil heard the man say something in French to his companion. What it was, of course, he did not understand. It did not escape his sharp eye that the canoe was approaching the spot where he stood—very slowly, it is true, but rapidly enough to be perceptible. He was too experienced a hunter to be taken off his guard, but he chose, for the present, not to appear aware of this suspicious circumstance.

"Well, my friend, you earned your escape, although I was sorry to lose you."

"Don't doubt it. Like to get me again, wouldn't you?"

"Ha! You choose to be facetious. If you will give yourself up, you shall be assured of honorable treatment, and shall receive a good, round sum of money."

"Rather guess not. Good-by—that canoe is coming rather closer than I fancy."

As the woodman turned to flee, the Frenchman discharged his pistol. His aim, however, was guided solely by the sound of voice, as he had not been able to obtain a glimpse of the American, after his escape from the canoe. As a natural consequence his shot sped wide of the mark.

After running a few rods, Veghte paused, and to his amazement he found that the Frenchman and savage had landed and were pursuing him. This discovery occasioned him little alarm, as he was now in his element—the forest; there he feared no foe. Had his fire-arms been in a serviceable condition, he would have made this pursuit the dearest the two men had ever attempted. He called out tauntingly to them and lured them to a considerable distance into the woods, when he performed a trick that we all can not help agreeing was decidedly a good one.

Taking a circuitous route, he came upon the creek again, at a point not a hundred yards distant from where the canoe of the Frenchman still lay. It required but a short time for him to discover the boat, and, when he did so, he entered it at once, and commenced paddling down-stream.

"That ar' is what I call a stroke of gen'us," mused Basil. "Only an American could 'riginate it. Frenchy, himself, wouldn't 've thought it; but, won't he do a heap o' swearing, when he finds it's me—Basil Veghte—that's run away with his man-o'-war?"

The delight experienced by the woodman was too great to be borne in silence, so he gave utterance to a series of whoops, that echoed through the woods, and rolled far out over Lake Erie on that still summer night.

It might be that the Frenchman began to suspect his liability of becoming the victim of a practical joke, or, perhaps, he was only aware of the foolishness of continuing a search in the wood for a woodman. Simultaneous with the demonstration of delight upon the part of the latter, his two enemies appeared upon the shore, very nearly opposite him.

"Hello, there!" called out the large man, as before.

Fortunately, at this portion the creek was of considerable width, so that Veghte had little or nothing to fear from the weapon in the hands of his foe. Nevertheless, he sent the canoe close under the opposite bank, so as to make as wide a range as possible.

"Wal, its hello again, and what's the row now?"

"What are you a doing in our canoe?"

"Going to take a little sail down to Presq' Isle."

"But you have no right to do that. That is not fair. The canoe belongs to us."

"I kinder feel as though I couldn't spare it."

"But that is not honorable. I should not have treated you so."

"I came here in this boat, Frenchy, didn't I?"

"Of course you did—of course."

"Then, of course, I go back in it."

"But—but this is not right—it is not as civilized nations should do—"

"Bah! shut up, you oncivilized fool! Prate to somebody that hain't sense! Come to Presq' Isle if you want to see me."

"I shall be there sooner than you think."

Basil Veghte paused to hear no more, but sent the light vessel skimming like a bird down the creek toward the lake. He knew that the garrison was in danger—that the dark storm so long gathering over it was now ready to burst. Strong arms and brave hearts were needed within the wooden walls of Presq' Isle—and none more than his.

The hour was now late, and he was anxious to reach the fort before daylight. The nights were the briefest of the year, and he was well aware that he had no time to spare. Accordingly he bent all his energies to the task before him, and very shortly debouched into the lake.

Here his progress was not so rapid, although it was by no means tardy. He half suspected that the two would attempt to pursue and head him off when he should land; but a moment's reflection showed him the absurdity of this, and he did not give it a second thought.

The night was very warm, the wind having completely died out. The woodman did not forget that he still had formidable enemies upon the lake, and it was very probable that they might be encountered. He was, therefore, more on the alert than usual. He had proceeded, perhaps, a half-mile or so, when his trained ear detected the dip of paddles. He instantly paused, and, at the same moment, a large canoe, filled with men, loomed vaguely through the darkness. There was no doubt regarding its identity, and Veghte pulled silently away from it. He was not observed, and the dreaded enemies shortly disappeared in the darkness. Feeling that the "coast" was now clear, Basil once more bent to his work, and rapidly neared the fort.

The stretch of water to be passed was longer than at first imagined, and, after a time, the adventurer paused a moment to rest. While situated thus, he observed that the moon was rising. The lateness of the hour at first inclined him to the belief that day was breaking; but the appearance of the red disk above the horizon shortly revealed his mistake. While looking in the direction of the luminary, he detected for the second time the dip of a paddle directly behind him. A thrill of alarm shot through him; he was certain his old enemies had discovered him. With the moonlight upon the lake, he might well have occasion for alarm, and he turned his startled gaze around, to be ready for any emergency.

To the woodman's astonishment, the paddling ceased; but, looking intently through the darkness, he discerned a small shadowy object that could be nothing but a canoe. Indistinct as was the view, it revealed that it was not the large one which he had met a few moments before. What could it be?

The occupant had ceased paddling, and remained motionless, apparently waiting the movements of the leading canoe.

"That ar' is what I call cur'ous!" muttered Veghte, as he held his paddle in his hand, and surveyed the suspicious object as well as possible under the circumstances. "There's somebody settin' in that concern, for

I can see his head. I'm watching him, and he's watching me, and what *does* it mean. If he wants fight, all he has to do is to say so; but if he goes in peaceable, he's only got to let me alone. When I'm cotched ag'in there'll be little more trouble than there was the last time."

Dipping his paddle gently into the water, he commenced gliding noiselessly onward. He could not have progressed a rod when he saw that the other canoe was also moving in the same line with himself.

"If that's yer idea, come on!" he muttered. "There's some red-skins as can handle the paddle a little better than myself, but I don't b'lieve you're one of them."

It looked very much as though he was attempting to escape the stranger, but he really meant it as a simple trial of speed. Calling into exercise all the strength and skill at his command, he glanced back with considerable interest to watch his success.

For a few moments, he gained; but, as soon as the second person became aware of what was intended, the intervening space was rapidly lessened, and do all he could, Basil Veghte was unable to increase it.

"That ar' is also cur'ous!" he exclaimed, rather sullenly, as he relapsed into his usual rate of progress. "I'll begin to think I've forgotten how to paddle, or else everybody can beat me. You're a red-skin—that's sart'in, for I haven't met the white man that I'll knock under to, and I don't expect to meet him very soon."

Veghte dallied in every manner with his strange pursuer; but it was impossible either to catch or to flee away from him. He maintained the same relative distance, evidently determined on dogging him to the fort. Realizing that he had already wasted too much time, he applied himself with renewed vigor, and shortly after his canoe touched the sand on the beach opposite Presq' Isle.

It was already growing light in the east when the woodman stepped upon the shore, and he was naturally anxious to reach the fort and communicate with Ensign Christie. He stood a moment, glancing around to see whether any new danger threatened, when he caught the sound of a footstep, and soon detected a figure stealthily approaching. "What do you want?" he demanded, determined that his experience of the previous few hours should not be repeated. The person addressed made no answer, but continued to advance until the astonished woodman saw that it was a woman.

"Who are you? What do you want?" he again demanded.

"Mariano—eh!" was the whispered reply.

"Women *is* queer things!" was the exclamation of Veghte, as he recognized the Indian girl, whom he had been the means of saving from death, the preceding winter. "I thought you was dead."

She made no reply, but signified for him to follow her. The woodman hesitated a moment, for he knew this was a common artifice by which the Indians had lured many a white man to destruction. But he could not believe that she meant him harm, and he therefore obeyed—reluctantly, it must be confessed. The Indian girl led the way up the bank and a short distance in the woods. Here, in a sheltered depression, the woodman observed the embers of a camp-fire.

"Who kindled that?" he demanded, starting back.

She appeared unable to speak the English language, and therefore replied in pantomime. Veghte gathered that her meaning was, that there was no one else in the vicinity whom he need fear. She pointed toward the block-house, then said:

"Injin! French!"

This, undoubtedly, meant that danger menaced Presq' Isle—a fact which Basil Veghte well understood by this time. He nodded to signify as much. She then went through somewhat the same demonstration, pointing toward the woodman himself as the object of danger. The latter acknowledged that that truth was already impressed upon his understanding. She began another demonstration that was perfectly incomprehensible to him, when she suddenly paused, listened, and motioned for him to depart at once. Veghte needed no urging to do this, for he had experienced an uneasy feeling ever since he had seen Mariano. Accordingly he left, muttering, as he did so:

"*Women is queer things!*"

CHAPTER XI.

A QUESTION ANSWERED.

The soul that warmed that frame, disdained
The tinsel gaud and glare that reigned
  Where men their crowds collect.
The simple fur, untrimmed, unstained,
  This forest-tamer decked.—A. B. STREET.

VEGHTE made his way to the block-house and was admitted by Ensign Christie, who was all questions and anxiety. In a hurried manner, he related all that we have required the two preceding chapters to give. When he had finished, the commandant said:

"A light was displayed in answer to the signal on the lake?"

"Yes, and that's what gets me. Who done it?"

"Who did indeed? That is the all-important question."

"Where is Horace Johnson?"

"In bed, and hasn't left it since your departure. I have kept an eye on him. He has had nothing to do with it."

"The only one I can fix on is that Swede, Alltof."

"Nothing the matter with him. Ah! I have it. It was no one in the block-house who displayed the light. It was that man who stood upon the shore, when you pushed off. He saw that we were suspicious, and took that plan of saying so."

"But it looked to me as though it came from the *upper part* of the block-house, instead of being on the ground."

"You might easily have made a mistake. No, I'm satisfied that no one inside of Presq' Isle communicated with those on the lake."

The woodman, after carefully weighing the matter in his mind, came to the same belief as Christie. For the present he concluded to withhold his suspicions regarding Johnson. The matter therefore was dismissed, and that of the probable attack upon the fort, and the means of defence, was taken up.

The surface of Lake Erie was anxiously scanned, as soon as the first gray of morning appeared. It was as clear as at the dawn of creation. The French and Indians had left the vicinity of Presq' Isle before there was any liability of their being seen. The shore was examined, and revealed the track of several strange feet, while there were other evidences to prove their presence during the night.

Johnson took his departure in the morning, smiling and pleasant, saying that he hoped to see all ere long, and advising them not to be frightened from the reports they heard, and not to fear an attack at all.

All will admit that the preceding night had been a most eventful one to Basil Veghte, and yet, of all the memories that clustered around it, there was one that stood out with more distinctness than any other—his interview with the Indian girl, Mariano. More than one regret had passed through his mind during the preceding months, and the thought that she must have perished so cruelly upon that terrible December night. She was preserved, through the mercy of God, but by what means? What meant her actions, both at that time and subsequently? Was she actuated by a friendly motive toward himself? Did she wish to save the Forest Garrison by warning them of the danger that hung over them, or was she prompted by simple feelings of humanity?

These questions, all relating directly to a person of the feminine gender, were beyond the power of solution by the simple-hearted woodman. They would constantly intrude themselves, but he resolved to put them away for the present, and attend entirely to the duties of his position—that of ascertaining, if possible, the precise nature of the peril impending over Presq' Isle.

At the suggestion of Ensign Christie, Basil went on a reconnoissance. Both believed a hostile force was at no great distance, and both were fully convinced that an attack might be expected daily, or, rather, nightly.

The woodman penetrated into the forest with his usual caution, keeping at no great distance from the lake. Although in a situation where all his wits were needed, he could not forbear thinking about the Indian girl. He was asking himself in vain the question he had asked so often before, when he was considerably startled by hearing his name pronounced in a cautious undertone. Turning around, he was astonished at seeing the object of his thoughts before him. She stood smiling, half-timidly, as if she enjoyed his surprise.

"You look alarmed!" she said, in a very good English.

If Basil Veghte was startled at seeing this creature before him, it may be safely said that he was amazed when he heard these words uttered. He could scarce believe his ears until she spoke again:

"Can you not speak? Why are you so frightened?"

"You're Mariano, that Injin gal, ain't you?"

"Yes."

"Heaven save me! When did you learn to talk?"

"Years ago, when I was a child."

"You ain't much else yit. Why didn't you talk last night, instead of going through them motions, that I couldn't be sure I understood?"

"I will tell you some time; I can not now. Why did you leave the block-house this morning?"

"I came out to see what I could l'arn about them French and Injins, that intend to attack us."

The girl now approached the woodman, looking to the right and left as she did so, as if to satisfy herself that no other eyes were looking upon her. Then she spoke in a low voice, that possibly could not have been overheard had an eavesdropper been within a few feet of them.

"They are coming," she said. "*They are gathering in the wood. They will come to-morrow!*"

Basil started back, for he was not prepared for this. He expected an assault or demonstration at some time, perhaps before the expiration of a week, but he was not dreaming that it would come as soon as this. He knew, from the manner in which the girl spoke, that she was uttering the truth only.

"How many of them?" he finally asked.

"Hundreds! They will burn down the place, as they did Sandusky."

"Women is queer things!" was the mental reply of the woodman. "How does she know about this?" Then aloud, "Why do you come to tell me this?"

A reproachful light filled the dark eyes of Mariano, and for a moment she did not answer. Then she spoke in that subdued, musical voice:

"You saved my life. Can I ever forget you?"

An indescribable emotion thrilled through the being of the woodman, at these words. He could not understand it, and for a moment was silent.

"Do you come to save me, or to save Ensign Christie and the rest of 'em?"

"Both; I would do any thing to save you."

Hardly conscious of what he did, Basil reached forward to draw the girl to him, but she deftly slid from his grasp.

"No, no," she said in a terrified manner.

"I didn't mean to hurt you!" he said unutterably mortified at the display of feeling upon his part.

"I know you would not hurt me for any thing in the world. What did you mean?"

"I—I—didn't—I didn't mean any thing."

"They want you!" she added, returning quickly to the subject that had first engaged them. "They want you; they will hunt the woods for you."

"Let 'em hunt," answered Basil, not conscious, perhaps, of a slight sense of superiority at his boast. "Let 'em hunt. I ain't afeard. I've been hunted all my life, and was never catched yet. It'll take a purty smart Frenchman or Injin to do it, too."

"You are skillful in the hunt."

The dark, nut-brown face of the woodman grew darker under this compliment, and he was abashed for a moment.

"I have spent thirty years in the woods, and I should have been a natural fool if I hadn't learnt *something* in that time."

Suddenly a thought of Johnson flashed over his mind.

"You remember that man who was with me upon that night I fetched you up to the camp-fire—Johnson was his name. Do you know him?"

Hesitating at first, she signified, by a motion of her head, that she did.

"He was in the block-house last night."

Her eyes dilated and she retreated a step, as if overcome with surprise or terror.

"What's the matter? Ain't he a friend to us?"

"Don't let him come again. He is very bad!"

"I thought so once, but kinder begun to think maybe I was mistook. You've knowed him a good while, I reckon. You knowed him that night of the storm, didn't you?"

"Yes."

"Why didn't you speak? He pretended he knowed nothing about you all the time."

"Had you not better go to the fort?" she asked, after a moment's hesitation, not heeding the remark.

"I s'pose I had. See here, you are a friend, ain't you?—and you don't think much of that Johnson, do you?"

"No, I can not like him."

"Then come with us to the block-house. Come there and live with us."

Basil Veghte made as if to go, but she did not offer to follow. He repeated his invitation with all the earnestness possible, but she shook her head.

"You will be safe."

"I can not think so; maybe I will come and live with your people some day."

She turned on her heel, and a moment later had disappeared in the wood. Basil stood a moment in deep thought.

"Women is queer things," he muttered. "I'd give a good deal if I knowed more about 'em. She said maybe she'd come and live with us people, some day. I wonder what she meant by it? Come and live with us. That sounds strange! Why can't she come now? There is something about her queerer than something about other women. Maybe I'll know some day. Well, women is queer things, that's sart'in."

The woodman set out on his return to the fort, meditating as he went. Stealthily making his way through the wood, he soon discovered himself in the presence of an Indian council. It required all the art of which he was master to approach near enough to obtain a view without exposing himself to observation. He found there were about two hundred Indians and a dozen or so white men. Among the former he noticed Balkblalk, and among the latter Mr. Horace Johnson, who seemed perfectly at home in the company.

Some chief whom he had never seen was haranguing the company in an excited manner. Although not able to comprehend the meaning of a single word uttered, it was easy to see it had reference to Presq' Isle. He continually pointed in that direction, gesticulating with great vehemence. His address seemed to please his auditors, who gave frequent exclamations of pleasure.

The French conversed together, but their tones were

so subdued that even their hum could not be overheard. It no doubt was imagination, but the woodman selected a dozen of the brawny sons of the wood, and several of the Frenchmen, as his pursuers the evening before. Little did they imagine that the man whom they were so anxious to secure was at that moment within sound of their voices.

Veghte waited a half-hour or so, when, judging he had seen sufficient, he fell back with great care, and, as soon as free, made all haste to the block-house. He lost no time in communicating all that had taken place to Ensign Christie, not omitting every word spoken by Mariano, the Indian girl. As may well be supposed, the commandant was now doubly anxious. The almost certainty of an attack on the morrow drove nearly every other thought from his mind. Still, before the day had passed, he found time to exchange a word or two with the honest-hearted woodman regarding the meaning of the words uttered by the Indian girl.

"Why, Basil, she *loves* you!" laughed Ensign Christie.

"Heavens! Do you think so?"

"Certainly. What makes you appear so frightened?"

"I don't know; but them women *is* queer things."

Little sleep visited the forest garrison of Presq' Isle that night. The watch was doubled, and all slept in the expectation of being called on every moment to repel an attack of the French and Indians.

CHAPTER XII.

THE CRISIS AND THE FALL.

*Meanwhile, for one moment, hand in hand,
We gaze in each other's eyes.*—OWEN MEREDITH.

On the fifteenth day of June, 1764, the blood-red cross of St. George floated over Presq' Isle; but the morning sun had not yet risen when shouts, yells, and the rapid discharge of guns, and the appearance of two hundred Indians, paint-bedaubed and furious, proclaimed that the day of trial was at hand.

At the first alarm Ensign Christie and his men abandoned the main body of the fort, and withdrew within the block-house as their citadal. There, with coolness and deliberation, they completed their preparations for repelling the assault.

The Indians swarmed together, under protection of the rising ground, and sent a tempest of bullets, fire-arrows, and burning pitch-balls upon the doomed block-house. Every loop-hole and crevice let in a constant stream of balls; and, were a head exposed but for a twinkling, it was the immediate target for a score of rifles.

The roof of the block-house was constructed of dry shingles, which were again and again set on fire; but, under cover of the bullet-proof planks, water was dashed upon it, and the fire was as often extinguished. Hour after hour the contest raged, without any decided advantage upon either side, when the Indians rolled logs to the top of the ridges, where they constructed three formidable breast-works, from behind which they could fire their shot and hurl their fire-balls with greater effect.

At this juncture the defenders saw the Indians throwing up stones and dirt behind one of their breastworks. This meant that they were seeking to undermine the fort—an insidious species of warfare, against which there was no defence. While many a cheek blanched at this appalling danger, another more imminent attracted their attention.

The hogsheads of water kept within the block-house for the purpose of extinguishing the fires were nearly emptied. There was a well on the parade-ground, but to approach it was certain death, as the Indians swept the space by a constant hurricane of balls. The only recourse was to dig a well in the block-house itself.

The floor was ripped up, and the grimy, panting men sprung to their work, while others, with their muskets so foul and hot that they nearly blistered their hands, continued discharging them through the loop-holes.

All blackened from the smoke of guns and copious perspiration, with the utmost anxiety marked on his countenance, Ensign Christie leaned over his men and encouraged them in their toilsome work of digging the well.

Very slowly to him, but, in reality, very rapidly, the men sunk below the surface of the ground. Every shovelful that was thrown up was scrutinized by the commandant. "Work, men, work, for all now depends upon you." The dirt is examined again; still no sign of water.

"The roof is on fire!" is called from above, in a husky voice. O heavens! and the well is not half completed. Dig, men, dig! Huge shovelfuls are thrown upward, but still the moist earth fails to yield water.

"The roof is on fire!—the shingles are blazing!" Ensign Christie frantically glances around, losing his presence of mind for a moment. Hark! Feet are heard tramping rapidly over the roof. What can it mean?

A hoarse cheer, half suppressed, but still exultant, arises from the garrison. At the second of extreme danger, Basil Veghte sprung out upon the roof, tore off the shingles amid the hurtling balls, and returned again, without so much as a scratch. All praise to the noble fellow!

Dig, men, dig, for the danger is staved off but a moment! The fire-arrows and burning pitch-balls are raining upon the roof again, and it already begins to smoke. Another such a rash exploit as that of the woodman can only result in death, for fifty loaded rifles stand waiting for his appearance.

Exhausted and worn out, the men come up from the well to rest themselves awhile by loading and firing their clogged rifles. Others go down and take their places, and the dirt is cast up more rapidly than ever.

Thank Heaven! water is struck, and not a moment too soon. Simultaneous with the bubbling of the fluid comes the alarming cry again: "The roof is on fire!" Hand the buckets down!—scrape up the mud and gravel and water! There!—pass it quickly! Once more the fire is drowned.

And now it is night. All day long, with scarcely a moment's intermission, the attack had raged. The Indians seemed to have resolved to wear out the obstinate defenders simply by exhausting them. While some sleep and rest, others keep up the assault with renewed fury and strength.

Even night brings no reprieve. The inky darkness is constantly lit up by the flashes of the guns, and the wearied garrison can snatch scarcely a moment's rest. With great apprehension they await the dawn of morning, for they know too well their implacable enemies have not been idle.

Hardly was it light when the garrison discovered that the subterranean approaches had been pushed within striking distance of the commandant's house, which stood on the parade, very close to the block-house. This was set on fire at once, and the pine-logs blazed up with scorching fierceness. It was a hot day in June, and this conflagration rendered the air within the block-house (already suffocatingly thick from the burning of powder) almost intolerable.

The outer wall of the block-house, from its exposure to the extreme heat, blistered, blackened, scorched, and then, in a dozen places, burst into flames. Water was passed up from the well, and the almost fainting soldiers succeeded in extinguishing it. The house, roaring, crackling and surging in each breath of wind, sunk down a mass of red-hot embers.

By this time, to use the words of Ensign Christie, in his official report, the men were "exhausted to the greatest extremity," yet there was no thought of yielding. The conduct of each man showed that there was no taint of treason in Presq' Isle.

All through the day, the men, staggering from weakness, continued to fire their guns from the dark, heated walls of the block-house, still hoping almost against hope. Not until midnight was there any cessation of hostilities, when some one called out from the entrenchments, that further resistance would avail nothing, as preparations were completed for firing the block-house both from above and below. Christie inquired whether there was any one who could speak English. Upon this, some one called out that if they yielded their lives would be spared, but if they continued to fight, they must be all burned alive. The commandant asked until morning to give an answer, and this being granted, the majority of his men sunk down into slumber while others maintained a watch until daylight.

After the lull in the firing, Christie encountered Veghte. Both were so begrimed and blackened that they scarcely recognized each other in the dim light of the block-house.

"Is that you, Basil? I hardly knew you. I'm afraid it's all up with us. What do you think?"

The woodman sat flat down upon the floor.

"If this infarnal old shell hadn't been built in such a place, we might 've fought 'em all summer."

"Its location is unfortunate, as Lieutenant Cuyler told us; but it is too late to talk about that now. They've been undermining us ever since last night, and they can burn us alive."

"Let 'em burn! Who cares!"

The commandant saw that Basil was excited, and he waited a few moments before he spoke.

"As long as there is a shadow of hope we shall not yield. If we are compelled to surrender, I shall not do so until our own terms are guaranteed me."

"Terms with French and Injins!" sneered the woodman. "What you talking about? They'll never give you terms!"

"Then we'll die together!" replied Christie, compressing his lips. "It is as well to burn first as last."

"What you going to tell 'em in the morning?" sullenly asked Veghte, after a moment's pause. "You promised to give 'em an answer, and you'll have to do it."

"Do you think it true that their preparations for burning the block-house are completed?"

"Can't tell, they're such liars; like 'nough they are, and like 'nough they ain't."

"I will send you and one of the men out to treat with them. When you go, you can look out and see whether they have spoken the truth. If they have, you may stipulate that our lives shall be spared, and we shall be given permission to retire to the nearest post. If they have spoken falsely, put them off with some pretext, get back into the fort if you can, and we'll blaze away again. Our men, you see, are all asleep and will have quite a rest."

This course of action seemed to strike the fancy of the woodman. He brightened up and spoke more cheerfully:

"You're game, Christie, that's sart'in."

"All our men are, and the Indians have learned it by this time, too. They know that any agreement we make will be lived up to the very letter."

"Will theirs?"

"That's hard to tell. The Indians can't be relied on, but the French can."

"Do you s'pose *they've* got much to say?"

"No; they've taken little part in the frontier-war so far as I can hear."

"They had plenty to say, when they tried to catch me in the lake, t'other night."

"They are a civilized people, and will conduct themselves according to the rules of honorable warfare. I hope, too, they will have some influence upon the others. We both need rest; let us sleep; the watches are provided."

The men sunk down upon the floor and slept soundly until morning. Then, as agreed upon, Basil Veghte and one of the soldiers advanced from the block-house to treat with their enemies. Before doing so the former agreed upon a private signal, by which he was to announce to Christie the truth regarding the assertion that they had the power to fire the block-house, in the effectual manner mentioned.

How anxiously Ensign Christe watched the movements of Basil Veghte and his companion as they advanced to meet the Indians. They had gone but a few rods, when the woodman turned deliberately around and surveyed the works of their assailants. He then made the signal agreed upon to the commandant, and, after parleying awhile, withdrew within the fort, announcing that Christie himself would come forth and make the conditions.

Ensign Christie advanced midway between the block-house and their breastworks, where he met two of their principal chiefs. They seemed to respect the white man for the gallantry displayed by him and his comrades, and solemnly agreed to spare the lives of all the garrison, and allow them to retire unmolested to the nearest post. The soldiers, grim, haggard, and wild, came forth, and in spite of the capitulation were instantly seized as captives. Shortly after they were sent to Detroit as prisoners, from which place Ensign Christie and Basil Veghte made their escape, and gained the fort of Detroit in safety.

Thus fell Presq' Isle, than which no fort along the frontier was more courageously defended.

CHAPTER XIII.

SALUS!

On the afternoon of a mild autumn day, in the year 1764, Basil Veghte was hunting along the northern shore of Lake Erie. He was alone, and had not met a white person for over a week—of red men he had seen an abundance. He had hovered around their camp-fires, not daring to expose himself, for, in this vast solitude, the two races encountered as implacable enemies.

The woodman appeared graver than usual; evidently he had some great burden upon his mind. He stood on the hard, compact sand of the beach, and the sullen waves came almost to his feet. He was leaning on his rifle, and looking out upon the broad lake, whose opposite boundary his eye could not reach. His gaze was that wandering, aimless one, which showed him to be lost in reverie. At intervals he drew a deep sigh, and poised himself first upon one foot and then upon another.

"Women *is* queer things!" he finally exclaimed. "There's no mistake; they git my time. I can understand an Ottawa, but I can't understand a female man—that is, a man that's a woman. They look as though they meant something, when they don't mean nothing, and don't look so when they mean something else. They never used to bother me when a boy, except when my good old mother—God bless her—whacked me with the broomstick. Ah, me! it's a pity that I ever found that gal, Mariano! It ain't a pity, neither, for she would have been froze if I hadn't—I mean—I'm a fool, that's it!" he exclaimed, petulantly, as he again shifted his position.

"Always to hunt—hunt—and scout for the forts. How come I to take to the woods in the first place? Here for years and years I've tramped along Lake Erie, till I feel like a fish out of water when I am in any other place. I hung around Presq' Isle so long it got to seeming like home; and then the place must be burned over my head. I've been to Detroit since Pontiac has left, but I never liked the looks of the place.

"And how is this going to end?" he asked himself, after a moment's pause. "I'm getting well on in years, and I've had white hairs in my head for a long time. I s'pose I shall hunt, hunt, tramp, tramp, till some day a red-skin wings me, or I go to sleep and never wake up again.

"Yes, I must wake up again—but where? In the other world, that I've thought about, dreamed about, and remember hearing my mother talk about, when I stood at her knee? I wonder whether I shall meet her, and the little sister that they put in the ground, a great many long years ago? Something tells me I shall—but it is wonderful—wonderful!"

The solemn thought precluded all others for a time, and the large tears trickled down the bronzed face of the scout.

"I've felt this way afore," he resumed, "but I didn't feel so bad as I do now. What makes it? Why, a *woman*."

The woodman was right. Many a sleepless night and unquiet day had he endured since encountering Mariano, on that awful December night. Thoughts that he had never allowed himself to entertain came unbidden, and would not depart. The forest life, although very dear and fascinating, lost part of its charms, from its contrast with *what might be!*

Home! with its charms and sacred joys—a place where to lay his head; a gentle form, with the love-light beaming in her eyes, waiting to welcome his return; the sweet word, "Father," uttered by infantile lips; the days of wandering ended, and rest, peace, repose!

Such was the picture painted on the blue sky, lit up by the stars overhead at midnight, and that floated in the air above, around him, at all times. And now, Basil Veghte stood on the shore of Lake Erie, comparing the real and the imaginary.

Could he change his ways? Could he give up the life at this late day that had become a second nature to him? Was it possible to settle down into a staid citizen of the colonies? The hunt, the scout, the thrill of the deadly encounter—the exultation of victory: *could* these be given over forever?

What the final answer to these questions would have been must forever remain unknown. For, while still absorbed in his reverie, his eye, not forgetful of its cunning, wandered to and fro at intervals, and suddenly detected upon the lake a single canoe, coming in a direct line toward him.

"Injin ag'in," he muttered, as he stepped back, and let the barrel of his rifle fall in the hollow of his left arm.

"There's but one of 'em," he added, after carefully surveying the approaching boat, "and he must be blind if he don't see me. What does he mean by coming right square ag'in' me? It can't be that he's friendly; for them kind are only met with near the settlements and forts."

The course of the canoe, beyond question, was in a straight line to the woodman. The single occupant had descried the white man, and was doubtless making all haste toward him.

"That's queer," said the latter, glancing uneasily behind him. "It can't be there's any one on the trail—no, I know there isn't. I'm in a bad piece of country, and I've been powerful careful for the last day or two. Howsumever, Sweetlove will send a bullet as far as the iron of any redskin, and I'll wait and be ready."

Straight ahead came the canoe, scarcely impeded by the waves upon which it rose and sunk like a cork. The Indian handled the paddle with matchless skill, and made no sign or signal to him who was watching his motions with such interest.

"Come on! It shan't never be said of Basil Veghte that he run from a single Injin—— God save me!"

The canoe, rising on the breast of a wave, discovered to the amazed gaze of the woodman, Mariano, the beautiful Ottawa. For a moment, the simple-hearted man was tempted to believe there was something supernatural in this sudden appearance of the object of his thoughts. Where could she have come from? How happened it that the two should encounter in this boundless solitude? It might happen, but the chances were as one in a million.

A second glance identified the girl beyond all question. A whirl of emotions went through him. His breath came fast, and for a few moments, he seemed to be actually contemplating retreat; but his iron will composed his countenance, and, with apparent calmness, he awaited the approach of the girl.

The canoe touched the sand, and, blooming and smiling, Mariano sprung lightly out and came forward to meet him.

"I knew you when I saw you standing here," remarked, as she looked up in his face with the familiar, trusting look of innocence.

"You did! Well, I would sooner have expected to meet my dead grandmother. Where are you going?"

"To Detroit."

The woodman looked into the beaming face before him. Strong emotions were surging through his breast, and strange words were forcing themselves to his lips; but, naturally enough, he pressed them back, to give way to more trivial ones.

"Where is Horace Johnson?"

"I do not know; I never want to meet him. I have fled away from him."

"What's the matter? Has he offered to hurt you? If he has, just say so. What has become of that Ottawa, Balkblalk?"

"He's dead; was killed at Presq' Isle. He was my father."

"You don't tell me! And Johnson was your husband?"

"No, but he wanted to be. Last winter Balkblalk carried me far into the woods, and when I would not say I would be that man's squaw, my father left me to die. You saved me."

"What made you go away that night from the camp-fire?"

"To get away from *him*. I heard my father call. He whistled for me. He was sorry he left me in the woods. He took me away. He would have killed you, if that man had not been with you."

"He never liked me, I know. There is one thing I never knowed for sart'in. I wish you would tell me."

She looked up in his face, waiting for his question.

"Was that Johnson a traitor to his own race?"

She answered rather hesitatingly, seeing the fire in her questioner's eye. "Balkblalk wanted him to be. He went into the fort to find out, but when he came out he did not tell any thing in my hearing."

"Where was he, when Presq' Isle fell?"

"I do not know for certain."

It was evident that Mariano did not desire to fan the flame of the scout's indignation against Johnson. Was it because she loved peace and hated bloodshed?

"When father was killed, I went to Canada to get away from that white man," she added, as if to avoid any misconstruction.

"Did he follow you?"

"Yes; he has pursued me until my life is hunted out of me." This was said with a feeling which betrayed how much she must have suffered.

"Are you going to live in Canada?"

"Yes; that's where I was born and lived. I am going to visit Detroit, to see good and wise white friends; then I shall return to my tribe, and never leave it."

Veghte looked at her a moment in tender admiration.

"You talk English better than I do."

"I talk it well, for I have been much in the settlements and in the missions. I only pretended not to understand it when we met before."

A silence now ensued that was painfully embarrassing to the woodman. Feeling desperate, he finally came to the point with a startling abruptness.

"You like me, Mariano?"

"I do." Her dark face lit up with a gleam of radiant joy—then it became very sad and pale.

"We are of different races. Could you be the wife of a white man—of a white man that really loved you?"

She was startled, and her pale face grew more pallid, as she replied with difficulty:

"No, I wish to be the wife of no man. I am but an Indian, and not worthy of a white man's home and love."

"Do not say this. You are worthy, if any woman is. *Can't* you be *my* wife?"

"No, no, no," she replied, excitedly. She was agitated; tears filled her eyes, and her resolution visibly wavered. But, it was only for a moment, Choking down her sensations with an effort, she said "good-by," stepped into her canoe, and paddled away. Sad and sorrowful, Basil Veghte watched the frail vessel till it finally disappeared far up the lake. Then, with a weary sigh, he turned and plunged into the wilderness.

THE END.

GEORGE ROUTLEDGE & SONS'
REWARD & PRESENTATION BOOKS.

In 4to, price 12s. 6d.

	s. d.
Naomi; or, The Last Days of Jerusalem. By Mrs. WEBB. With Steel Plates.	12 6
The Prince of the House of David. With 60 Illustrations.	

In 8vo, price 10s. 6d.

Discoveries and Inventions of the Nineteenth Century. By ROBERT ROUTLEDGE, B.Sc., F.C.S., Assistant Examiner in Chemistry and Natural Philosophy to the University of London, and J. H. PEPPER, late of the Polytechnic. With numerous Illustrations. — 10 6

The Young Lady's Book. By the Author of "A Trap to Catch a Sunbeam." An entirely New Book of Occupations, Games, and Amusements for Young Ladies. With 300 Illustrations and Coloured Plates.

The Adventures of Captain Hatteras. By JULES VERNÉ. 1. THE ENGLISH AT THE NORTH POLE. 2. THE FIELD OF ICE. 220 Illustrations by RIOU.

The Sunlight of Song. With Original Music by BARNBY, ARTHUR SULLIVAN, and other eminent living Composers. Original Illustrations by the most eminent Artists, engraved by DALZIEL Brothers.

In small 4to, cloth gilt, price 8s. 6d.; gilt edges, 9s. 6d.

Every Boy's Book. A New Edition. Edited by EDMUND ROUTLEDGE. A Complete Cyclopædia of Sport and Recreation. With 100 Illustrations and 9 Coloured Plates. — 8 6

In 4to, and royal 8vo, cloth gilt and gilt edges, price 7s. 6d. each. Illustrated by the best Artists.

Grimm's Household Stories. With 220 Plates. — 7 6

Homes and Haunts of the British Poets. By WILLIAM HOWITT. With many Illustrations.

Little Barefoot. A Domestic Tale. By BERTHOLD AUERBACH. With many Illustrations.

A New Book by **Auerbach.** With 300 Illustrations.

Household Tales and Fairy Stories. With 380 Illustrations by J. D. WATSON, HARRISON WEIR, and others.

Christmas Carols. Set to Music. With Original Illustrations by the Brothers DALZIEL.

SEVEN-AND-SIXPENNY BOOKS, *continued.*

s. d.
7 6 **Bonnechose's France.** A New Edition. 1872.

The Language of Flowers. By the Rev. ROBERT TYAS. With 12 pages of Coloured Plates by KRONHEIM.

Longfellow's Poetical Works. With Plates by JOHN GILBERT. Author's Complete Edition. Demy 8vo, cloth, gilt edges.

Bunyan's Pilgrim's Progress. With 100 Plates by J. D. WATSON.

Popular Natural History. By the Rev. J. G. WOOD, M.A. With Hundreds of Illustrations.

National Nursery Rhymes. Set to Music by J. W. ELLIOTT. With Original Illustrations, engraved by DALZIEL Brothers.

Naomi; or, The Last Days of Jerusalem. By Mrs. WEBB. With Steel Plates. Post 8vo, cloth, gilt edges.

Dante's Divine Comedy. Translated by H. W. LONGFELLOW. 1 vol., crown 8vo, cloth.

Hogg on the Microscope. With 500 Illustrations and 8 Coloured Plates.

Andersen's Stories for the Household. 8vo, cloth, gilt edges, with 220 Illustrations.

Robinson Crusoe. With 110 Plates by J. D. WATSON.

Sheridan Knowles' Dramatic Works.

In cloth, gilt edges, 6s. each.

6 0 **Routledge's Every Boy's Annual for 1876.** Edited by EDMUND ROUTLEDGE. With many Illustrations, and beautiful Coloured Plates.

Shipwrecks and Disasters at Sea. By W. H. G. KINGSTON. With more than 100 Illustrations.

The Adventures of Robinson Playfellow, a Young French Marine. With 24 Plates, and many Woodcuts.

Bab Ballads. By W. S. GILBERT. With Illustrations by the Author.

Travelling About. By Lady BARKER. With Six Plates and 5 Maps.

Pepper's Boy's Play-book of Science. 400 Plates.

D'Aulnoy's Fairy Tales. Translated by PLANCHÉ.

Perrault's Fairy Tales. Translated by PLANCHÉ, &c.

Pepper's Play-book of Mines, Minerals, and Metals. With 300 Illustrations. Post 8vo, gilt.

JUVENILE BOOKS. 5

Six-Shilling Books, *continued*.

                                                                             s. d.

Motley's Rise of the Dutch Republic. Crown 8vo, cloth, gilt.   6 0

An Illustrated Natural History. By the Rev. J. G. Wood, M.A. 500 Illustrations.

The Playfellow. By Harriet Martineau. With Coloured Plates.

The English at the North Pole. By Jules Verné. 129 Illustrations by Riou.

The Field of Ice. By Jules Verné. 129 Illustrations by Riou.

The Adventures of Johnny Ironsides. 115 Plates.

ROUTLEDGE'S BRITISH POETS.
Edited by Rev. R. A. Willmott.
Illustrated by Birket Foster, Sir John Gilbert, &c.

Chaucer's Canterbury Tales. Illustrated by Corbould.   5 0

Kirke White. Illustrated by Birket Foster.

Southey's Joan of Arc, and Minor Poems.

Herbert. With Life and Notes by the Rev. R. A. Willmott.

Longfellow's Complete Poetical Works. With Illustrations. Fcap. 8vo.

Burns' Poetical Works. Illustrated by John Gilbert.

Fairfax's Tasso's Jerusalem Delivered. Illustrated by Corbould.

Crabbe. Illustrated by Birket Foster.

Moore's Poems. Illustrated by Corbould, &c.

Byron's Poems. Illustrated by Gilbert, Wolf, Foster, &c.

Campbell's Poetical Works. Illustrated by W. Harvey.

Lover's Poetical Works. With a Portrait.

Rogers' Poetical Works. With a Portrait.

Dryden's Poetical Works. With a Portrait, &c.

Mrs. Hemans' Poems.

Lord Lytton's Poetical Works.

Lord Lytton's Dramatic Works.

GEORGE ROUTLEDGE & SONS'

ROUTLEDGE'S FIVE-SHILLING JUVENILE BOOKS.

In fcap. 8vo and post 8vo, gilt, Illustrated by GILBERT, HARVEY, FOSTER, and ZWECKER.

s. d.
5 0 Children of the New Forest. By *Marryat*.
Little Savage. By *Marryat*.
History of British India.
Lilian's Golden Hours. By *Silverpen*.
Boy's Treasury of Sports and Pastimes.
The Queens of Society.
The Wits and Beaux of Society.
Entertaining Knowledge.
Pleasant Tales.
Extraordinary Men and Women.
Dora and her Papa. *Author of "Lilian's Golden Hours."*
Great Battles of the British Army.
The Prince of the House of David.
The Pillar of Fire.
The Throne of David.
The Story of the Reformation. By *D'Aubigné*.
Popular Astronomy and Orbs of Heaven.
Once upon a Time. By *Charles Knight*.
White's History of England.
The Winborough Boys. By *Rev. H. C. Adams*.
The Prairie Bird. By *Hon. C. Murray*.
The Great Sieges of History. With Coloured Plates.
Cooper's Leatherstocking Tales.

Great Battles of the British Navy. With Coloured Plates.
Memoirs of Great Commanders. With Coloured Plates.
The Family Arabian Nights. Coloured Plates.
The Adventures of Robin Hood. With Coloured Plates.
Holiday Stories. By *Lady Barker*.
Half Hours with the Best Letter Writers. By *C. Knight*.
Characteristics of Women. By *Mrs. Jameson*.
Memoirs of Celebrated Female Sovereigns. By Mrs. *Jameson*.
What Men have said about Woman.
British Heroes in Foreign Wars. By *James Grant*. With Coloured Plates.
Don Quixote for Boys. With Coloured Plates by Kronheim.
Wroxby College. By *Rev. H. C. Adams*.
Boys. By *Lady Barker*.
Sunday Evenings at Home By *Rev. H. C. Adams, M.A.* First Series.
―― Second Series.
Memoirs of Celebrated Women. By *G. P. R. James*.
Nine Little Goslings. By *Susan Coolidge*. With Illustrations.

JUVENILE BOOKS.

ROUTLEDGE'S FIVE-SHILLING BOOKS

	s. d.
Little Wide-Awake for 1876. By Mrs. SALE BARKER. With 400 Illustrations and Coloured Frontispiece.	5 0

Grimm's Fairy Tales. With Coloured Plates. Crown 8vo, gilt.

Hans Andersen's Stories and Tales. 80 Illustrations, and Coloured Plates.

Walter Crane's Picture Book. With 64 pages of Coloured Plates. Cloth, gilt edges.

Country Life. Illustrated by Poetry, and 40 Pictures by BIRKET FOSTER.

What the Moon Saw, and other Tales. By HANS C. ANDERSEN. With 80 Illustrations, and Coloured Plates.

Chimes and Rhymes for Youthful Times. With Coloured Plates. (Uniform with "Schnick-Schnack.")

Buds and Flowers. A Coloured Book for Children. (Uniform with "Schnick-Schnack.") Small 4to, cloth.

Schnick-Schnack. Trifles for the Little Ones. With Coloured Plates. Small 4to, cloth.

Buttercups and Daisies. A new Coloured Book for Children. (Uniform with "Schnick-Schnack.") Small 4to, cloth.

Watts' Divine and Moral Songs. With 108 Woodcuts, engraved by COOPER.

Original Poems for Infant Minds. By JANE and A. TAYLOR. With Original Illustrations by the Best Artists, engraved by J. D. COOPER.

Little Lays for Little Folk. Selected by J. G. WATTS. With Original Illustrations by the best living Artists, engraved by J. D. COOPER. 4to, cloth, gilt edges.

The Picture Book of Reptiles, Fishes, and Insects. By the Rev J. G. WOOD, M.A. With 250 Illustrations. 4to, cloth.

——————— **Birds.** By the Rev. J. G. WOOD, M.A. With 242 Illustrations. 4to, cloth.

——————— **Mammalia.** By the Rev. J. G. WOOD, M.A. With 250 Illustrations. 4to, cloth.

Happy Day Stories for the Young. By Dr. DULCKEN. With full-page Plates by A. B. HOUGHTON.

ROUTLEDGE'S FIVE-SHILLING BOOKS.

In super-royal 8vo, cloth gilt, price 5s.

s. d.
5 0 **Walter Crane's Picture Book.** Containing 64 pages of Pictures, designed by WALTER CRANE, viz.:—"Luckie-boy's Party," "The Old Courtier," "How Jessie was Lost," "The Fairy Ship," "Chattering," "Annie and Jack in London," "Grammar in Rhyme," "The Multiplication Table in Verse."

Walter Crane's New Toy Book. Containing 64 pages of Pictures, designed by WALTER CRANE, viz.:—"Cinderella," "My Mother," "The Forty Thieves," "The Three Bears," "One, Two, Buckle my Shoe," "Puffy," "This Little Pig," "Noah's Ark A B C."

Goody Two-Shoes Picture Book. Containing "Goody Two-Shoes," "Beauty and the Beast," "A B C of Old Friends," and "The Frog Prince." With 24 pages of Coloured Plates from designs by WALTER CRANE.

The Henny-Penny Picture Book. Containing "Henny-Penny," "Sleeping Beauty," "Baby" and "The Peacock at Home." With 24 pages of Coloured Plates.

The Poll Parrot Picture Book. Containing "Tittums and Fido," "Reynard the Fox," "Anne and her Mamma," and "The Cats' Tea Party."

Routledge's Coloured A B C Book. Containing "The Alphabet of Fairy Tales," "The Farm Yard Alphabet," "Alphabet of Flowers," and "Tom Thumb's Alphabet."

My Mother's Picture Book. Containing "My Mother," "The Dogs' Dinner Party," "Little Dog Trusty," and "The White Cat." Large 4to, cloth.

The Red Riding-Hood Picture Book. Containing "Red Riding Hood," "Three Bears," "Three Kittens," and "Dash and the Ducklings." Large 4to, cloth.

Our Nurse's Picture Book. Containing "Tom Thumb," "Babes in the Wood," "Jack and the Beanstalk," and "Puss in Boots." Large quarto, cloth.

The Child's Picture Book of Domestic Animals. 12 Large Plates, printed in Colours by KRONHEIM. Large oblong, cloth.

The Child's Picture Book of Wild Animals. 12 Large Plates, printed in Colours by KRONHEIM. Large oblong, cloth.

Pictures from English History. 63 Coloured Plates by KRONHEIM. Demy 4to, cloth.

JUVENILE BOOKS. 9

FIVE-SHILLING BOOKS, *continued.*

                                                                                           s. d.

Routledge's Scripture Gift Book. Containing "The   5 0
Old Testament Alphabet," "The New Testament Alphabet," "The History of Moses," and "The History of Joseph." Demy 4to, cloth.

Routledge's Picture Gift Book. Containing "Nursery Songs," "Alphabet of Trades," "Nursery Tales," and "This Little Pig."

The Pet Lamb Picture Book. Containing "The Toy Primer," "The Pet Lamb," "The Fair One with Golden Locks," and "Jack the Giant Killer."

The Robinson Crusoe Picture Book. Containing "Robinson Crusoe," "Cock Sparrow," "Queer Characters," and "Æsop's Fables."

ROUTLEDGE'S FOUR-AND-SIXPENNY JUVENILES.

A New Series of Juvenile Works.

All well Illustrated, and bound in an entirely New Binding, expressly designed for them.

LIST OF THE SERIES.

Life of Richelieu. By *W. Robson.*
Monarchs of the Main. By *Walter Thornbury.*
Roger Kyffyn's Ward. By *W. H. G. Kingston.*
The Man o' War's Bell. By *Lieut. C. R. Low.*
The Orville College Boys. By *Mrs. Henry Wood.*
Wonderful Inventions. By *John Timbs.*
Æsop's Fables. With Plates by *H. Weir.*
The Illustrated Girl's Own Treasury.

The Boy's Own Country 4 6
Book. By *Miller.*
The Forest Ranger. By *Major Campbell.*
Pleasures of Old Age.
Tales upon Texts. By the *Rev. H. C. Adams.*
Pictures from Nature. By *Mary Howitt.*
Stephen Scudamore the Younger. By *A. Locker.*
Hunting Grounds of the Old World.
Watch the End. By *Thomas Miller.*

In fcap. 8vo, cloth, gilt edges, price 4s. each.

Every Girl's Book. By Miss LAWFORD. With many 4 0
Illustrations.

Every Little Boy's Book. By EDMUND ROUTLEDGE. With many Illustrations.

ROUTLEDGE'S THREE-AND-SIXPENNY REWARD BOOKS.

With Coloured Illustrations, gilt sides.

s. d.
3 6 Robinson Crusoe.
Sandford and Merton.
Evenings at Home.
Swiss Family Robinson.
Edgeworth's Popular Tales.
———— Moral Tales.
———— Parent's Assistant.
———— Early Lessons.
The Old Helmet. By the Author of "*The Wide, Wide World.*"
The Wide, Wide World.
Edgar Clifton.

The Lamplighter.
Melbourne House.
Queechy.
Ellen Montgomery's Bookshelf.
The Two Schoolgirls.
The Pilgrim's Progress.
Gulliver's Travels.
Andersen's Fairy Tales.
The Arabian Nights.
The Adventures of Robin Hood.
Don Quixote for Boys.
Captain Cook's Voyages.

All the above have Coloured Plates.

MAYNE REID'S JUVENILE BOOKS.

In fcap. 8vo, cloth gilt, with Illustrations.

3 6 Bruin.
The Boy Tar.
The Desert Home.
Odd People.
Ran away to Sea.
The Forest Exiles.
The Young Yägers.

The Young Voyageurs.
The Plant Hunters.
The Quadroon.
The War Trail.
The Bush Boys.
The Boy Hunters.

ANNE BOWMAN'S JUVENILE BOOKS.

With Plates, fcap. 8vo, cloth gilt.

3 6 The Boy Voyagers.
The Castaways.
The Young Nile Voyagers.
The Boy Pilgrims.
The Boy Foresters.
Tom and the Crocodiles.
Esperanza.

The Young Exiles.
The Bear Hunters.
The Kangaroo Hunters.
Young Yachtsmen.
Among the Tartar Tents.
Clarissa.
How to make the Best of It.

www.ingramcontent.com/pod-product-compliance
Lightning Source LLC
Chambersburg PA
CBHW020830190426
43197CB00037B/1341